Cambridge Elements

Elements in Non-local Data Interactions: Foundations and Applications
edited by
Luca Calatroni
French Centre of Scientific Research (CNRS)

LATENT MODES OF NONLINEAR FLOWS

A Koopman Theory Analysis

Ido Cohen
Technion – Israel Institute of Technology
Guy Gilboa
Technion – Israel Institute of Technology

CAMBRIDGE
UNIVERSITY PRESS

CAMBRIDGE
UNIVERSITY PRESS

Shaftesbury Road, Cambridge CB2 8EA, United Kingdom

One Liberty Plaza, 20th Floor, New York, NY 10006, USA

477 Williamstown Road, Port Melbourne, VIC 3207, Australia

314–321, 3rd Floor, Plot 3, Splendor Forum, Jasola District Centre, New Delhi – 110025, India

103 Penang Road, #05–06/07, Visioncrest Commercial, Singapore 238467

Cambridge University Press is part of Cambridge University Press & Assessment, a department of the University of Cambridge.

We share the University's mission to contribute to society through the pursuit of education, learning and research at the highest international levels of excellence.

www.cambridge.org
Information on this title: www.cambridge.org/9781009323857
DOI: 10.1017/9781009323826

First published 2023

A catalogue record for this publication is available from the British Library.

ISBN 978-1-009-32385-7 Paperback
ISSN 2755-1296 (online)
ISSN 2755-1288 (print)

Latent Modes of Nonlinear Flows

A Koopman Theory Analysis

Elements in Non-local Data Interactions: Foundations and Applications

DOI: 10.1017/9781009323826
First published online: May 2023

Ido Cohen
Technion – Israel Institute of Technology

Guy Gilboa
Technion – Israel Institute of Technology

Author for correspondence: Ido Cohen, idoc@campus.technion.ac.il

Abstract: Extracting the latent underlying structures of complex nonlinear local and nonlocal flows is essential for their analysis and modeling. In this Element the authors attempt to provide a consistent framework through Koopman theory and its related popular discrete approximation – dynamic mode decomposition (DMD). They investigate the conditions to perform appropriate linearization, dimensionality reduction, and representation of flows in a highly general setting. The essential elements of this framework are Koopman eigenfunctions (KEFs) for which existence conditions are formulated. This is done by viewing the dynamic as a curve in state-space. These conditions lay the foundations for system reconstruction, global controllability, and observability for nonlinear dynamics. They examine the limitations of DMD through the analysis of Koopman theory and propose a new mode decomposition technique based on the typical time profile of the dynamics.

Keywords: nonlinear decomposition, dynamic mode decomposition, homogeneous operators, gradient flows, nonlinear spectral theory, Koopman eigenfunctions, Koopman mode decomposition

ISBNs: 9781009323857 (PB), 9781009323826 (OC)
ISSNs: 2755-1296 (online), 2755-1288 (print)

Contents

1 Introduction

Knowing the latent space of certain data allows one to represent it concisely and to differentiate between signal and clutter parts. Recovering this space in a data-driven manner is a long-standing research problem. Data resulting from dynamical systems is represented commonly as spatial structures (modes) that are attenuated or enhanced with time. A common technique in linear flows is *separation of variables*. It is assumed that a solution $u(x,t)$ of a linear flow can be expressed as

$$u(x,t) = X(x)T(t). \tag{1.1}$$

That is, the solution is a multiplication of a function of the spatial variable x and a function of the temporal variable t. In this study we examine, from various angles, the following paradigm: a *nonlinear flow* can be well approximated (or even exactly expressed) by a linear combination of variable separated functions,

$$u(x,t) \approx \sum_{i=1}^{m} X_i(x)T_i(t). \tag{1.2}$$

In this context, the spatial structures X_i are referred to as *modes* and T_i are *time-profiles*. For such an approximation, if the error is negligible and m is small, we obtain a significant simplification of the system. This enables better understanding and modeling, allowing accurate interpolation and prediction of the dynamics.

The theory of Koopman argues that for many nonlinear systems data measurements evolve as if the dynamical system is linear (in some infinite-dimensional space). A well-known algorithm to approximate these measurements is *Dynamic Mode Decomposition* (DMD) of Schmid (2010). In this work, we formulate sufficient and necessary conditions for the existence of these measurements. These findings highlight certain flaws of DMD. Finally, we suggest a new mode decomposition to overcome some of these problems, originated in an algorithm for general spectral decomposition of Gilboa (2018).

In many dynamical processes, there are measurements of the observations that evolve linearly, or approximately so; see Otto and Rowley (2021). A theoretical justification for that can be traced back to the seminal work of Koopman (1931). These measurements are referred to as *Koopman Eigenfunctions* (KEFs). An algorithm was proposed by Mezić (2005), *Koopman Mode Decomposition* (KMD), to reconstruct the dynamics using spatial structures, termed as modes, which are the coefficients of Koopman eigenfunctions. Since KEFs evolve as if they were observations in a linear dynamical system, KMD can interpret the original dynamics as a linear one.

This decomposition might be infinite-dimensional. In Schmid (2010) it was suggested to approximate KMD in a finite domain. If the KEFs measurements are linear combinations of the observations then DMD yields the Koopman mode accurately. As noted in Kutz et al. (2016a), DMD can be interpreted as an exponential data-fitting algorithm. That is, DMD generally detects well the spatial components $X_i(x)$ in Eq. (1.2) if the time-profiles $T_i(t)$ are of the form $e^{\lambda_i t}$. In the more general nonlinear case, DMD may not reveal well the underlying modes and the dynamics.

Recently the authors and colleagues have formalized this insight in Cohen et al. (2021a), in the context of homogeneous flows, referring to it as the DMD paradox. As the step size approaches zero, dynamic reconstruction with DMD results in positive mean squared error but, paradoxically, with zero DMD error. In general, this paradox exists in any dynamical system whose KEFs are not linear combinations of the observations. This phenomenon becomes extreme when the system is zero-homogeneous, as shown in Cohen et al. (2021b). Such cases are common in gradient flows of one-homogeneous functionals, such as local or nonlocal TV-flows; see Andreu et al. (2001) and Gilboa and Osher (2009). In that case, the dynamics is only in C^0 almost everywhere and exponential decay is a very crude and inaccurate approximation. For such flows, lifting the observations to a finite higher-dimensional space does not solve the problem (see, for example, Korda and Mezić [2018]; Williams et al. [2015a]).

Even though KMD may exist, DMD may not recover the dynamic and yield unsatisfactory results; see Cohen et al. (2021a). This alleged contradiction between KMD and DMD leads us to examine the fundamentals of Koopman theory. We follow the general solution of a KEF with respect to time and analyze the mapping between the state-space and the time variable. The existence of this mapping depends on the smoothness properties of the dynamics. As a direct result, we introduce a new method that overcomes the DMD limitations for smoothing-type processes. These findings, with some adaptations, are valid in the full continuous settings, as discussed by Kutz et al. (2016b) and Mauroy (2021).

Main Contributions We formulate the conditions for the existence of a KEF. If it exists, there is an infinite set of KEFs. We distinguish between different types of eigenfunction groups and analyze their multiplicity. We show that certain multiplicities are crucial to obtain dynamics reconstruction, controllability, and observability (Section 4). These conclusions are extended to the full continuous setting. Conditions for the existence of *Koopman Eigenfunctionals* (KEFals) are presented (Section 5). Following these insights, we suggest an alternative algorithm for finding Koopman modes induced by fitting time profiles that best characterize the dynamics. This algorithm overcomes some inherent limitations of DMD (Section 6). We attempt to bridge between nonlinear spectral decomposition and KMD. Specifically, we show that spectral *Total Variation* (TV) of Gilboa (2014) and its generalizations yield Koopman modes. Throughout this work, we illustrate the theory with simple toy examples. Additional examples and experiments are given in Section 7. In the following section, we provide the essential definitions and notations.

2 Preliminaries

In this section, we present some background on the Koopman operator, its eigenfunctions and eigenfunctionals, and the related DMD framework. We note certain properties of variational calculus that are relevant to Section 5. In addition, we outline the work of Gilboa (2018) and Katzir (2017), where nonlinear flows are decomposed through a dictionary of decay profiles. We adapt this method for the extraction of Koopman modes in Section 6.

2.1 Koopman Theory

2.1.1 Discrete Spatial Setting

We consider a dynamical system in a semidiscrete setting, that is, the spatial variable x is a finite dimension (belongs to $\mathbb{R}^N$) and the time variable t is continuous in the range $[a, b]$ expressed as

$$\frac{d}{dt}\boldsymbol{x}(t) = P(\boldsymbol{x}(t)), \quad \boldsymbol{x}(0) = \boldsymbol{x}_0 \in \mathbb{R}^N, \quad t \in I, \tag{2.1}$$

where $\boldsymbol{x} \in \mathbb{R}^N$ is a state vector, $P\colon \mathbb{R}^N \to \mathbb{R}^N$ is a (nonlinear) operator, and $I = [a, b] \subseteq \mathbb{R}^+$ is a time interval. Let $g\colon \mathbb{R}^N \to \mathbb{R}$ be a measurement of $\boldsymbol{x}$. The Koopman operator K_P^τ is a linear operator that acts on the infinite-dimensional space of measurements $g(\boldsymbol{x})$ of the state, defined by Koopman (1931) and Mezić (2005) as

$$K_P^\tau(g(\boldsymbol{x}(s))) = g(\boldsymbol{x}(s+\tau)), \quad s, s+\tau \in I, \tag{\textbf{KO}}$$

where $\tau > 0$. The Koopman operator is linear; namely, it admits

$$K_P^\tau(\alpha g(\boldsymbol{x}(s)) + \beta f(\boldsymbol{x}(s))) = \alpha K_P^\tau(g(\boldsymbol{x}(s))) + \beta K_P^\tau(f(\boldsymbol{x}(s)))$$

for all measurements g and f and for all constants α and β. In addition, the Koopman operators $\{K_P^\tau\}_{\tau \geq 0}$ admit a semigroup property, more formally,

$$K_P^{\tau_2} \circ K_P^{\tau_1} = K_P^{\tau_1+\tau_2},$$

where $\circ$ denotes the composition operator. An eigenfunction of the Koopman operator, $\varphi(\boldsymbol{x})$, admits

$$K_P^{\tau}(\varphi(\boldsymbol{x}(s))) = \varphi(\boldsymbol{x}(s+\tau)) = \eta^{\tau}\varphi(\boldsymbol{x}(s)), \quad s, s+\tau \in I, \tag{2.2}$$

for some $\eta \in \mathbb{C}$. Due to the semigroup attribute of the Koopman operator, the following limit exists:

$$\begin{aligned}\lim_{\tau\to 0}\frac{K_P^{\tau}(\varphi(\boldsymbol{x}(s))) - \varphi(\boldsymbol{x}(s))}{\tau} &= \lim_{\tau\to 0}\frac{\varphi(\boldsymbol{x}(s+\tau)) - \varphi(\boldsymbol{x}(s))}{\tau} \\ &= \frac{d}{dt}\varphi(\boldsymbol{x}(t))\bigg|_{t=s}.\end{aligned} \tag{2.3}$$

This limit can be explained by the relations of the Koopman operator and Lie derivatives; see Brunton et al. (2021). It can be shown (see, for instance, Mauroy et al. [2020], p. 10) that a KEF admits

$$\frac{d}{dt}\varphi(\boldsymbol{x}(t)) = \lambda\cdot\varphi(\boldsymbol{x}(t)), \quad \forall t \in I, \tag{2.4}$$

for some $\lambda \in \mathbb{C}$. The relation between η in Eq. (2.2) and λ in Eq. (2.4) is $\eta = e^{\lambda}$. The solution of this linear ODE is given by

$$\varphi(\boldsymbol{x}(t)) = \varphi(\boldsymbol{x}(a))e^{\lambda t}, \quad \forall t \in I. \tag{2.5}$$

Koopman Mode Decomposition *Koopman Mode Decomposition* (KMD) is a spatiotemporal mode decomposition of dynamical systems based on KEFs. Namely, the state-space $\boldsymbol{x}$ can be expressed as (Mezić [2005])

$$\boldsymbol{x}(t) = \sum_{i=1}^{\infty}\boldsymbol{v}_i\varphi_i(t), \tag{2.6}$$

where $\varphi_i(t)$ is a KEF (a real function) and $\boldsymbol{v}_i$ is the corresponding vector (in $\mathbb{R}^N$), referred to as Koopman mode. When the dynamic is nonlinear, the decomposition may have infinite elements. In practice, a finite approximation method is used. The most common one is DMD, as explained in Section 2.2.

2.1.2 Full Continuous Setting

Let $u : L \subset \mathbb{R}\times I \subseteq \mathbb{R}^{+} \to \mathbb{R}$ be the solution of the following PDE:

$$u_t(\mathrm{x},t) = \mathcal{P}(u(\mathrm{x},t)), \quad u(\mathrm{x},0) = f(\mathrm{x}). \tag{2.7}$$

We assume that u belongs to a Hilbert space $\mathcal{H}$ with an inner product $\langle v,u\rangle$ and its associated norm $\|\cdot\| = \sqrt{\langle\cdot,\cdot\rangle}$. $\mathcal{P} : \mathcal{H} \to \mathcal{H}$ is a (nonlinear) operator.

Let $Q: \mathcal{H} \to \mathbb{R}$ be a proper, lower-semicontinuous functional. The Koopman operator, $K^{\tau}_{\mathcal{P}}$, in the sense of PDE, is defined by Nakao and Mezić (2020) as

$$K^{\tau}_{\mathcal{P}}(Q(u(\mathrm{x}, s))) = Q(u(\mathrm{x}, s + \tau)), \quad s, s + \tau \in I. \tag{2.8}$$

An eigenfunctional, ϕ, of the Koopman operator is a functional admitting the following:

$$K^{\tau}_{\mathcal{P}}(\phi(u(\mathrm{x}, s))) = \phi(u(\mathrm{x}, s + \tau)) = \eta^{\tau}\phi(u(\mathrm{x}, s)), \quad s, s + \tau \in I. \tag{2.9}$$

By letting $\tau \to 0$, an eigenfunctional of the Koopman operator admits the following ODE:

$$\frac{d}{dt}\phi(u(\mathrm{x}, t)) = \lambda\phi(u(\mathrm{x}, t)), \tag{2.10}$$

for some $\lambda \in \mathbb{C}$. The relation between η in Eq. (2.9) and λ in Eq. (2.10) is $\eta = e^{\lambda}$. Thus, a *Koopman Eigenfunctional* (KEFal) is of the following form:

$$\phi(u(\mathrm{x}, t)) = \phi(u(\mathrm{x}, a))e^{\lambda t}, \quad \forall t \in I. \tag{2.11}$$

Koopman Mode Decomposition In the same manner as in the semidiscrete setting, we formulate the solution of the PDE, Eq. (2.7), with KEFals (Nakao and Mezić [2020]). Namely, the solution $u(x, t)$ can be expressed as

$$u(\mathrm{x}, t) = \sum_{i=1}^{\infty} d_i(\mathrm{x})\phi_i(t), \tag{2.12}$$

where $\phi_i(t)$ is a KEFal and $d_i(x)$ is the spatial mode. One way to approximate these spatial modes is by the method introduced by J. Nathan Kutz et al. (2018).

2.2 Dynamic Mode Decomposition

Dynamic Mode Decomposition (DMD) extracts the main spatial structures in the dynamics; see Schmid (2010). Backed by Koopman theory, DMD is a principal method to approximate the Koopman modes. It is a data-driven method, based on snapshots (mostly, uniformly in time) of the dynamics, $\boldsymbol{x}_k = \boldsymbol{x}(t_k)$. The main steps in DMD and its extensions (e.g. Exact DMD, Tu et al. [2013]; tlsDMD, Hemati et al. [2017]; fbDMD, Dawson et al. [2016]; S-DMD, Cohen et al. [2021a]; and optimized DMD, Askham and Kutz [2018]) are as follows:

1. *Dimensionality reduction* – finding the dominant parts of the dynamics.
2. *Linear mapping* – finding a linear mapping in the reduced dimensional space.
3. *Dynamic reconstruction* – expanding the dynamic back to the data space.

The result of DMD and its variants is sets of *modes* $\{\boldsymbol{\phi}_i\}$, *eigenvalues* $\{\mu_i\}$, and *coefficients* $\{\alpha_i\}$, where $i = 1,\ldots,r$ and r is the reduced dimension. The modes contain the spatial information, and the eigenvalues the temporal information. The modes are normalized to one ($\|\boldsymbol{\phi}_i\| = 1$), and the coefficients are the amplitudes. In the DMD framework, the dynamics is approximated by

$$\tilde{\boldsymbol{x}}_k \approx \sum_{i=1}^{r} \alpha_i \mu_i^k \boldsymbol{\phi}_i. \tag{2.13}$$

In what follows, we describe the DMD steps in detail.

Main Steps of Dynamic Mode Decomposition

Dynamic Mode Decomposition is a robust tool in dynamical system analysis. It has been applied on fluid mechanics, disease modeling, neuroscience, robotics, and finance; see Kutz et al. (2016a). This method is very applicable, since it is a fully data-driven algorithm, where no prior knowledge of the model is required. There are three main steps in DMD. The first is *dimensionality reduction*, representing the data in a lower-dimensional space. The second is *linear mapping*, finding the best linear dynamic that explains the data evolution in the lower-dimensional space, or, more precisely, finding the best linear dynamic that explains the data coordinates. The third is *dynamic reconstruction*, reconstructing the dynamic as an expansion of the lower-dimensional approximation. In the rest of this section, we summarize the classic DMD first introduced by Schmid (2010).

Dimensionality Reduction Given N observations of the dynamical system, Eq. (2.1), we form the data matrices as

$$X_0^{M-1} = [\boldsymbol{x}_0, \boldsymbol{x}_1, \ldots, \boldsymbol{x}_{M-1}], \quad X_1^M = [\boldsymbol{x}_1, \boldsymbol{x}_2, \ldots, \boldsymbol{x}_M] \in \mathbb{R}^{N\times M}, \tag{2.14}$$

where $\boldsymbol{x}_k = \boldsymbol{x}(t_k)$. To find the spatial structures, the *Singular Value Decomposition* (SVD) is applied on the data matrix,

$$X_0^{M-1} = U\Sigma V^*, \tag{2.15}$$

where V^* is the conjugate transpose of V. The columns of U span the column space of X_0^{M-1}. Thus, the spatial structures are represented by its coordinates:

$$\boldsymbol{c}_k = U^* \boldsymbol{x}_k. \tag{2.16}$$

Assume the data is embedded in subspace spanned by the first r columns of U. Then, the coordinates related to that subspace are

$$\boldsymbol{c}_{r,k} = U_r^* \cdot \boldsymbol{x}_k. \tag{2.17}$$

Linear Mapping Now, we would like to find the linear mapping from $\boldsymbol{c}_{r,k}$ to $\boldsymbol{c}_{r,k+1}$. The objective function we would like F to minimize is

$$||F \cdot C_{r,0}^{M-1} - C_{r,1}^{M}||_{\mathcal{F}}^{2}, \tag{2.18}$$

where $||\cdot||_{\mathcal{F}}$ denotes the Frobenius norm and

$$C_{r,0}^{M-1} = U_r^* X_0^{M-1}, \quad C_{r,1}^{M} = U_r^* X_1^{M}. \tag{2.19}$$

We call this objective function the *DMD error*.

Then, we can write either the recurrence relation of the coordinates as

$$\boldsymbol{c}_{r,k+1} \approx F \cdot \boldsymbol{c}_{r,k}, \tag{2.20}$$

or the coordinate dynamic in general as

$$\boldsymbol{c}_{r,k} \approx F^{k} \cdot \boldsymbol{c}_{r,0}. \tag{2.21}$$

Dynamic Reconstruction The last step is to reconstruct the dynamic by returning to the data space. Based on (2.16), one can reconstruct a sample at step k from its coordinates as

$$\tilde{\boldsymbol{x}}_k = U_r \boldsymbol{c}_{r,k}. \tag{2.22}$$

The entire dynamic can be reconstructed as

$$\tilde{\boldsymbol{x}}_k \approx A \tilde{\boldsymbol{x}}_{k-1}, \tag{2.23}$$

where $A = U_r \cdot F \cdot U_r^*$. Please note that $U_r^* U_r = I$. The rank of matrix A is r at most. Therefore, the approximated solution of the dynamic $\tilde{x}_k$ is a linear combination of r eigenvectors of A that decays exponentially according to the corresponding eigenvalues.

Modes, Eigenvalues, and Coefficients The DMD result is the set of eigenvectors of A, referred to as *modes*, the corresponding *eigenvalues*, and *coefficients*:

Modes are defined as $\Phi = \begin{bmatrix} \boldsymbol{\phi}_1 & \cdots & \boldsymbol{\phi}_r \end{bmatrix}$, where $A\phi_i = \mu_i \phi_i$.

Eigenvalues are the diagonal entries of the matrix D, $\{\mu_i\}_{i=1}^{r}$.

Coefficients are defined by $\boldsymbol{\alpha} = \begin{bmatrix} \alpha_1 & \cdots & \alpha_r \end{bmatrix}^T = \Phi^T \boldsymbol{x}_0$.

We can now reconstruct the approximate dynamics as

$$\hat{\boldsymbol{x}}_k \approx \Phi D^k \alpha = \sum_{i=1}^{r} \alpha_i \mu_i^k \boldsymbol{\phi}_i. \tag{2.24}$$

This formulation is known as the DMD reconstruction of the dynamics.

Reconstruction Error Many applications are satisfied with the preceding step for recovering the spatial structures in the dynamics. However, for recovering the dynamics with DMD, another measurement must be considered. To assess the accuracy, not only should the "moving" from one sample to the next one be taken under consideration but also the dynamic in general. Namely, the criterion should be the summation over the distance between x_k and $\hat{x}_k$. For example, the summation over squared Euclidean distances results in

$$E_{rec} = \sum_{k=0}^{M} \|x_k - \hat{x}_k\|^2 = \|X - \hat{X}\|_{\mathcal{F}}^2, \tag{2.25}$$

which is the Frobenius norm of the error.

2.3 Homogeneous Spectral Decomposition and Typical Decay Profiles

Asymptotic behavior of dynamical systems (Aubry et al. [1991]) plays a key role in either decomposition or analysis; see Mauroy et al. (2013). It was applied on a wide range of applications (e.g. Giannakis and Majda [2012]). This method is applicable in the general context of any spatiotemporal signal.

In recent years, new spatiotemporal decomposition methods have been developed for homogeneous dynamical systems (when P in Eq. (2.1) admits $P(av) = a|a|^{\gamma-1}P(v), \forall a \in \mathbb{R}$). The spatiotemporal decomposition of the dynamic is assumed to be (either a finite or an infinite) summation of spatial modes associated with the typical decay profile of the dynamic. The decay profile is the temporal factor of the dynamic $T(t)$, where it is initialized with an eigenfunction of the operator P. Thus, generally, the solution splits into different parts decaying according to the same profile but at different paces.

2.3.1 Decay Profile

Let $P(\cdot)$ be a γ-homogeneous operator ($\gamma \in \mathbb{R}$) over some Banach space $\mathcal{B}$. Let $\phi \in \mathcal{B}$ be an eigenfunction of P, admitting $P(\phi) = \lambda\phi$ for a real-valued λ. Then, the solution of the PDE (Cohen and Gilboa [2018, 2020]),

$$\frac{d}{dt}u = P(u), \quad u(t = 0) = \phi, \tag{2.26}$$

is given by

$$u(t) = a(t)\phi, \tag{2.27}$$

where

$$a(t) = \begin{cases} \left[(1 + \lambda(1-\gamma)t)^+\right]^{\frac{1}{1-\gamma}} & \gamma \neq 1, \\ e^{\lambda t} & \gamma = 1, \end{cases} \tag{2.28}$$

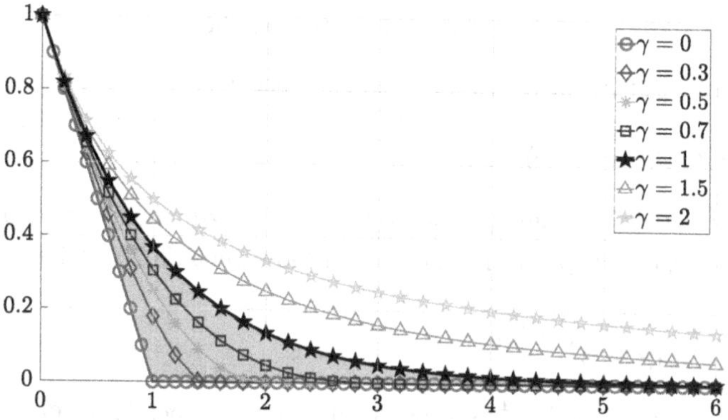

Figure 2.1 Typical decay profile of a γ-homogeneous flow. The temporal part in a variable-separated solution of a γ-homogeneous flow ($a(t)$ in Eq. (2.27)), initialized with a corresponding eigenfunction (Eq. (2.28)).

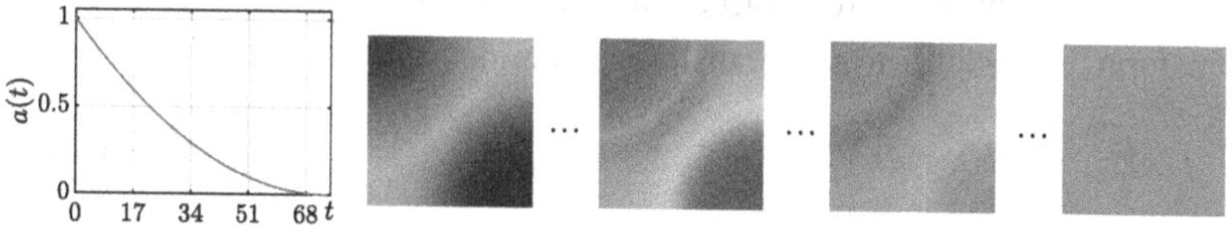

(a) Decay profile (b) $T = 0$ (c) $T = 12$ (d) $T = 28$ (e) $T = 74$

Figure 2.2 The solution of $u_t = \Delta_p u$ initialized with an eigenfunction ($p = 1.5$, $\lambda = -0.0269$). **(a)** The decay profile, Eq. (2.28), **(b)–(e)** snapshots of the solution, $u(t)$, at different time points. Spatially, the structure is fully preserved, where only contrast is diminishing with time until complete extinction. (Copyright ©2021 Society for Industrial and Applied Mathematics. Reprinted with permission. All rights reserved.)

and $(\cdot)^+ = \max\{\cdot, 0\}$. If P is a negative subgradient of a positive functional (such as the p-Dirichlet energy), the eigenvalue λ is negative for any nontrivial eigenfunction ϕ. The evaluation of (2.26), where P is the p-Laplacian operator and ϕ is a corresponding eigenfunction, is depicted in Fig. 2.2. The influence of the homogeneity on the decay profile is demonstrated in Fig. 2.1. In general, the solution reaches steady state in finite time when $\gamma \in [0, 1)$, the gray region in Fig. 2.1. The extinction time, T_{ext}, for which the dynamic vanishes is

$$T_{ext} = \frac{1}{\lambda(\gamma - 1)}. \tag{2.29}$$

The decay profile is essential in understanding signal processing frameworks related to eigenfunctions of γ-homogeneous operators, $\gamma \in [0, 1)$.

2.3.2 p-Spectral Decomposition

Transform Let $u(t)$ be a solution of a homogeneous PDE,

$$\frac{d}{dt}u = P(u), \quad u(t=0) = f, \tag{2.30}$$

where f is an arbitrary initial condition, and P is a γ-homogeneous operator, where $\gamma \in (0,1)$. The p-transform of Cohen and Gilboa (2020) is defined as

$$\phi(x,t) = \frac{t^\beta}{\Gamma(\beta+1)} D^{\beta+1}\{u(x,t)\}, \tag{2.31}$$

where $\beta = 1/(1-\gamma)$, $D_{b^-}^{\beta+1}$ is a fractional derivative operator of order $\beta + 1$ with respect to t, and $\Gamma(\cdot)$ is the extension of the factorial function to the real axis (for a positive integer n, we have $\Gamma(n) = (n-1)!$).

Inverse-Transform A reconstruction of the initial condition f from the p-transform, termed the inverse-transform, is defined as

$$\hat{f}(x) = \int_0^\infty \phi(x,t)dt. \tag{2.32}$$

Filtering The inverse-transform is the integral of the transform over the positive time axis. Thus, filtering can be defined as a weighted summation of the transform (analogous to Fourier filtering). More formally, the filtered signal, with respect to a (real-valued) filter $h(t)$, is given by

$$f_h(x) = \int_0^\infty \phi(x,t) \cdot h(t)dt. \tag{2.33}$$

Spectrum A spectrum admitting a Parseval-type identity is defined for the p-transform by

$$S(t) = \langle f, \phi(t) \rangle. \tag{2.34}$$

For further details regarding the p-framework, we refer the reader to Cohen and Gilboa (2020). This work follows the zero homogeneous spectral decomposition introduced in Gilboa (2014) and was thoroughly investigated in Burger et al. (2016), Bungert et al. (2019a), and Cohen et al. (2021b).

2.4 General Spectral Decomposition

One of the main goals of signal analysis is to represent a signal sparsely, yet precisely. We focus here on approximating a solution to a PDE, (2.7), by a decomposition of the form

$$u(\mathrm{x},t) \approx \sum_{i=1}^{L} h_i(\mathrm{x})a_i(t), \tag{2.35}$$

where $\{h_i(\cdot)\}_{i=1}^{L}$ are spatial functions and $\{a_i(t)\}_{i=1}^{L}$ are their respective time profiles. The time profiles are typical to the operator $\mathcal{P}$ and, for homogeneous operators, can be expressed analytically; see Cohen and Gilboa (2018). In the semidiscrete setting, the approximate solution of Eq. (2.1) can be expressed as

$$\boldsymbol{x}(t) \approx \sum_{i=1}^{L} \boldsymbol{v}_i a_i(t), \tag{2.36}$$

where $\{\boldsymbol{v}_i\}_{i=1}^{L}$ are spatial structures and $\{a_i(t)\}_{i=1}^{L}$ are the corresponding time profiles. Note that in some cases (e.g. linear diffusion or TV flow, as shown in Burger et al. [2016]) Eqs. (2.35) and (2.36) reach equality for finite or infinite L, respectively.

This is the basis of the general spectral decomposition suggested in the thesis of Katzir (2017) and summarized in Gilboa (2018, chapter 9). The initial condition of Eq. (2.7) is reconstructed with spatial structures that decay according to a known time profile. More formally, given the solution, $u(x,t)$, the spatial structures are the vectors of the minimizer (the vectors of the matrix $\mathcal{H}$) of the following optimization problem:

$$\min_{\mathcal{H}} \|\mathcal{U} - \mathcal{H}\mathcal{D}\|_{\mathcal{F}}^2, \tag{2.37}$$

where $\mathcal{U}$ is a matrix of the sampled solution in time and space, $\mathcal{H}$ is a matrix containing (in its columns) the main spatial structures, and $\mathcal{D}$ is a dictionary of decay profiles. One can formulate these matrices as

$$\mathcal{U} = \begin{bmatrix} u(\mathrm{x}_1,t_0) & \cdots & u(\mathrm{x}_1,t_M) \\ \vdots & & \vdots \\ u(\mathrm{x}_N,t_0) & \cdots & u(\mathrm{x}_N,t_M) \end{bmatrix}, \mathcal{H} = \begin{bmatrix} h_1(\mathrm{x}_1) & \cdots & h_r(\mathrm{x}_1) \\ \vdots & & \vdots \\ h_1(\mathrm{x}_N) & \cdots & h_r(\mathrm{x}_N) \end{bmatrix},$$
$$\mathcal{D} = \begin{bmatrix} a_1(t_0) & \cdots & a_1(t_M) \\ \vdots & & \vdots \\ a_r(t_0) & \cdots & a_r(t_M) \end{bmatrix}, \tag{2.38}$$

where $\mathcal{U} \in \mathbb{R}^{N\times(M+1)}$, $\mathcal{H} \in \mathbb{R}^{N\times r}$, and $\mathcal{D} \in \mathbb{R}^{r\times(M+1)}$. The optimization problem, Eq. (2.37), also fits the form of the semidiscrete setting in the dynamics of Eq. (2.1), where it is sampled in the time axis. We can formulate the following optimization problem:

$$\|X - \mathcal{V}\mathcal{D}\|_{\mathcal{F}}^2, \tag{2.39}$$

where the matrix X contains the samples of the dynamics

$$X = \begin{bmatrix} \boldsymbol{x}_0 & \boldsymbol{x}_1 & \cdots & \boldsymbol{x}_M \end{bmatrix} \in \mathbb{R}^{N\times(M+1)}, \tag{2.40}$$

the matrix $\mathcal{V}$ contains the main spatial structure of the dynamic (Eq. (2.36))

$$\mathcal{V} = \begin{bmatrix} \boldsymbol{v}_1 & \boldsymbol{v}_2 & \cdots & \boldsymbol{v}_r \end{bmatrix} \in \mathbb{R}^{N\times r}, \tag{2.41}$$

and the dictionary, $\mathcal{D}$, remains unchanged.

2.5 Variational Calculus

In this section, we recall some basic identities and properties from variational calculus that are necessary to the analysis of KEFs and KEFals.

2.5.1 Brezis Chain Rule

Let Q be a functional over some Banach space and ∂Q be its variational derivative. Under the regime of the PDE, Eq. (2.7), we can formulate the time derivative of the functional, $Q(u(t))$, through the "chain rule of Brezis" (Brezis [1973]) as

$$\frac{d}{dt}Q(u(x,t)) = \langle \partial Q(u), \frac{d}{dt}u(x,t)\rangle = \langle \partial Q(u), \mathcal{P}(u(x,t))\rangle. \tag{2.42}$$

2.5.2 Fréchet Differentiability

The operator $\mathcal{P} : \mathcal{H} \to \mathcal{H}$ is Fréchet differentiable at u if there exists a bounded linear operator $\mathcal{L}$ such that

$$\lim_{\|h\|\to 0} \frac{\|\mathcal{P}(u+h) - \mathcal{P}(u) - \mathcal{L}(h)\|}{\|h\|} = 0 \tag{2.43}$$

holds from any $h \in \mathcal{H}$. In this case, $\mathcal{P}(u+h)$ can be expanded in the Landau notation as

$$\mathcal{P}(u+h) = \mathcal{P}(u) + \mathcal{L}(h) + o(h), \tag{2.44}$$

where $\lim_{\|h\|\to 0} \|o(h)\|/\|h\| = 0$.

2.5.3 Proper Operator

The operator $\mathcal{P}(f)$ is proper if its norm gets a finite value for any $f \in \mathcal{H}$, $\|\mathcal{P}(f)\| < \infty, \forall f \in \mathcal{H}$.

2.5.4 Region of Attraction

Let $\boldsymbol{x}^*$ be an equilibrium point of the dynamical system in Eq. (2.1). The region of attraction is the largest set in $\mathbb{R}^N$ that admits the following property: if the initial condition of the dynamics is from the set, then the system converges to x^* (see e.g. Valmorbida and Anderson [2017]). More formally,

$$\mathcal{RA}(x^*) = \{x_{init} \in \mathbb{R}^N | x(t=0) = x_{init}, \lim_{t\to\infty} x(t) = x^*\}. \tag{2.45}$$

3 Motivation for This Work

Dynamic Mode Decomposition (DMD) has become a common tool in dynamical system analysis. This decomposition provokes interest in many domains of research, such as fluid dynamics, video processing, epidemiology, neuroscience, and finance; see Kutz et al. (2016a). A main advantage is its simplicity and the ability to often simplify complex processes by a few modes.

This Element attempts to present a critical investigation of such mode decomposition techniques. We highlight the differences and gaps between DMD and Koopman modes. The theoretical foundation of Koopman theory (and hence of DMD) is based on Koopman eigenfunctions. Thus, establishing conditions for the existence of such eigenfunctions is crucial for understanding the limitations of DMD. The linear eigendecomposition inherent in DMD further restricts its ability to characterize nonlinear flows well. We show that even a trivial example of a single mode with a linear time-profile decay is not modeled well by such methods. We then present connections to nonlinear spectral decomposition techniques, such as spectral total variation of Gilboa (2014). Finally, we suggest ways to overcome some of the noted limitations and present a decomposition based on time-profile dictionaries.

This work follows previous related studies, some of them performed in our research group. Cohen et al. (2021a) attempted to directly apply Koopman operator theory for homogeneous smoothing flows. Common nonlinear flows in image processing, such as TV-flow and p-Laplacian flows, were investigated. It was found that DMD cannot be naively applied in order to obtain appropriate modes. We recap the essentials of these findings in the following discussion.

3.1 The DMD Paradox

The DMD paradox was introduced in Cohen et al. (2021a) when the authors attempted to apply the DMD on homogeneous flows. Basically, DMD is an exponential data-fitting algorithm. Therefore, if the data does not decay exponentially, the modes and the dynamic reconstruction obtained by DMD can be fundamentally inaccurate. As an example, finite extinction time is inherent in flows where the homogeneity of the operator is $\gamma \in [0, 1)$ (for instance, see Eq. (2.29)). This induces an unavoidable error in DMD reconstruction.

For a single eigenfunction as the initial condition, sampling the solution with fixed step size dt, we get a rank-one data matrix. Thus, the only valid DMD decomposition is when the dimensionality reduction is maximal ($r = 1$). In that case, the DMD error, Eq. (2.18), converges to zero as $dt \to 0$. However, the reconstruction error, Eq. (2.25), is bounded from below.

A solution to this problem, suggested in Cohen et al. (2021a), is to formulate a time-rescaled *Partial Differential Equation* (PDE) that on one hand does not change the eigenfunctions and on the other hand decays exponentially. Thus, the spatial decomposition does not change and the decay profile of the dynamic transforms to exponential. Practically, this time rescaling is equivalent to homogeneity normalization, namely, the new dynamic is one homogeneous flow after time rescaling. This time rescaling is equivalent to adaptive (non-uniform) time sampling of the original flow. For further discussion on time rescaling we refer the reader to Giannakis (2019) in the context of Koopman operator analysis, and particularly to time rescaling (adaptive step size) of p-Laplacian flow in Cohen et al. (2019) in the context of numerical analysis. However, for nonsmooth zero-homogeneous flows more sophisticated techniques should be applied.

3.2 Discontinuous Dynamical Systems

The analytic solution of (2.30) for $\gamma = 0$ is known when the Banach space is $\mathbb{R}^N$ (see Burger et al. [2016] and Cohen et al. [2021b]). Applying the homogeneity normalization on zero-homogeneous flow, we find discontinuity in the dynamical modes. Thus, DMD is not valid when the solution is not smooth with respect to the time variable. The time rescale of (2.30) and the relation of DMD to zero-homogeneous decomposition are detailed in Cohen et al. (2021b).

3.3 Eigenvalue Multiplication

Dynamic Mode Decomposition is an exponential data-fitting algorithm; see Askham and Kutz (2018). Thus, DMD can recover precisely the dynamics only when the typical decay profile of the system is exponential. However, even for the limited case of exponential decays, DMD is not guaranteed to recover the dynamics. Let us consider a dynamic with a solution of the form

$$\boldsymbol{x}(t) = \boldsymbol{v}\left(e^{\lambda_1 t} + e^{\lambda_2 t}\right). \tag{3.1}$$

This solution cannot be reconstructed by a linear decomposition, since the mode v is associated with two eigenvalues, λ_1 and λ_2.

The rest of this Element attempts to propose a comprehensive solution to the aforementioned problems. We analyze the conditions for the existence of Koopman eigenfunctions and formulate the KMD modes. Since DMD is an approximation of KMD, if the KEFs do not exist, the approximation with DMD no longer has a theoretical justification. After formulating the DMD limitations, we propose an alternative mode decomposition, which coincides with KMD modes in a much broader setting.

4 Koopman Eigenfunctions and Modes

Koopman theory provides a linear representation to nonlinear dynamics by defining a new coordinate system. These coordinates are measurements in the state-space referred to as the Koopman Eigenfunction (*KEF*). In what follows, we discuss the basic terminology, settings, and application of Koopman operator theory.

We first lay out the settings of the system and provide sufficient and necessary conditions for the existence of KEFs. We show how to find KEFs and apply this for *Reconstruction of Conservation Laws*. We discuss the issue of KEFs' multiplicity and define a finite subset of independent KEFs, referred to as the *Ancestors*. The *Ancestor* set is the basis for reconstructing the dynamic and for measuring observability and controllability of the system. The section concludes by presenting *Koopman Mode Decomposition* (KMD), where some of its limitations are discussed.

4.1 Koopman Eigenfunctions

We first set the necessary degree of smoothness of P required to develop the theory. This setting is highly nonrestrictive and accommodates most useful linear and nonlinear dynamics for both local and nonlocal settings. In this section we examine the semidiscrete setting and the operator $P\colon \mathbb{R}^N \to \mathbb{R}^N$ in the dynamical system (3).

4.1.1 Settings of the Dynamical System

Assumption 4.1 (Piecewise Continuous P) The operator $P\colon \mathbb{R}^N \to \mathbb{R}^N$ is in C^0 a.e. with zero Dirac measures.

This leads to the following lemma.

Lemma 4.2 (Continuous solution $\boldsymbol{x}(t)$) *If the operator P in Eq.* (2.1) *admits Assumption 4.1, then the solution,* $\boldsymbol{x}$, *is in* C^1 *a.e.*

Proof The solution of the dynamics is

$$\boldsymbol{x}(t) = \boldsymbol{x}(a) + \int_a^t P(\boldsymbol{x}(\tau))d\tau. \tag{4.1}$$

The solution $\boldsymbol{x}(t) \in C^1$ *a.e.*, since $P \in C^0$ *a.e.* and does not contain Dirac measures. □

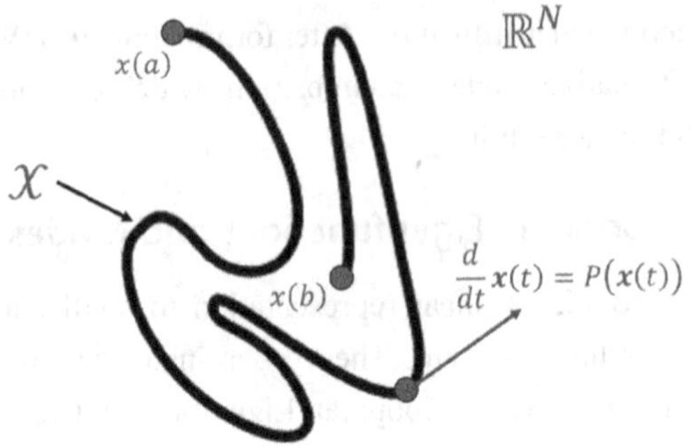

Figure 4.3 The dynamic solution is represented as a curve.[1]

The solution $\boldsymbol{x}(t)$, $t \in I \subset \mathbb{R}^+$, maps from the time range I to $\mathbb{R}^N$. It can be interpreted as a parametric curve in $\mathbb{R}^N$, where its tangential velocity is $P(\boldsymbol{x})$. Let us denote the path of $\boldsymbol{x}(t)$ as $\mathcal{X}$; this yields the trajectory of the system in $\mathbb{R}^N$, where the initial condition is $\boldsymbol{x}_0$ and $t \in I$. In Fig. 4.3 an illustration of the solution of a dynamical system is shown. Using the Kinematics analogy, we can say the dynamics is a mass going from $\boldsymbol{x}(a)$ to $\boldsymbol{x}(b)$ with the instantaneous velocity $P(\boldsymbol{x}(t))$, for every $t \in I$. We note that Lemma 4.2 holds also if Assumption 4.1 is limited to $\mathcal{X}$.

4.1.2 Necessary and Sufficient Conditions for KEFs

We now turn to discuss necessary and sufficient conditions for the existence of a nontrivial Koopman eigenfunction (that is, a nonzero function that admits Eq. (2.4) with $\lambda \neq 0$).

Proposition 4.3 (Condition for the inexistence of a Koopman eigenfunction) *If there is an equilibrium point in I, then a nontrivial Koopman eigenfunction does not exist.*

Proof Let $t_0 \in I$ be an equilibrium point and $\varphi(\boldsymbol{x}(t))$ be a Koopman eigenfunction. Then, $\boldsymbol{x}(t) = const$, $\forall t \in [t_0, b]$. Therefore, Eq. (2.4) does not hold for nontrivial φ for any $\lambda \neq 0$. □

Remark 4.4 (Finite support time dynamics) Let $P(\boldsymbol{x})$ define a dynamic for which the solution has a finite support in time. Namely, there is an extinction time point, T_{ext}, for which $P(\boldsymbol{x}(t)) = \mathbf{0}$, $\forall t \geq T_{ext}$. Then, if $T_{ext} \in I$, a

[1] The curve image is taken from `https://mathinsight.org/definition/simple_curve`.

Koopman operator K_P^τ has no eigenfunctions. We observe here that the time interval I is crucial for the existence or nonexistence of eigenfunctions.

4.1.3 KEF Formulation

A Koopman eigenfunction is a measurement of the solution $\boldsymbol{x}$ that admits Eq. (2.4) on the curve $\mathcal{X}$. As recently was stated in Bollt (2021), a Koopman eigenfunction can be formulated as an exponential function, where its argument is the inverse mapping from $\mathcal{X}$ to I. The formal definition of the mapping is as follows.

Definition 4.5 (Time state-space mapping) Let $\boldsymbol{x}(t)$ be the solution of the dynamical system (2.1) where $t \in I$. Let $\xi: \mathcal{X} \rightarrow I$ be a time state-space mapping from $\boldsymbol{x}$ to t,

$$t = \xi(\boldsymbol{x}). \tag{4.2}$$

This mapping is possible if the curve $\mathcal{X}$ is simple and open. (Simple, means the velocity is not zero, $\|d\boldsymbol{x}/dt\| \neq 0$, and open means injective). Necessary conditions for a curve to be simple are discussed, for instance, in Chuaqui (2018) and the references therein.

Lemma 4.6 (Differentiation of time state-space mapping) *Let the conditions of Lemma 4.2 hold. If the time state-space mapping, $t = \xi(\boldsymbol{x})$, exists, then it admits the following:*

$$\nabla\xi(\boldsymbol{x})^T P(\boldsymbol{x}) = 1 \quad a.e. \text{ in } \mathcal{X}. \tag{4.3}$$

Proof The mapping $\xi(\boldsymbol{x})$ is in C^1 a.e. in $\mathcal{X}$ since $\boldsymbol{x}(t) \in C^1$ *a.e.* in I. The time derivative of the mapping is

$$1 = \frac{d}{dt}t = \frac{d}{dt}\xi(\boldsymbol{x}) = \nabla\xi(\boldsymbol{x})^T \frac{d\boldsymbol{x}}{dt} = \nabla\xi(\boldsymbol{x})^T P(\boldsymbol{x}). \tag{4.4}$$

This expression is valid almost everywhere. □

Lemma 4.7 (Koopman eigenfunctions induced by a time state-space mapping) *Let the conditions of Lemma 4.2 hold and $\boldsymbol{x}(t)$ be the solution of Eq. (2.1). If there exists a time state-space mapping, $t = \xi(\boldsymbol{x})$, then a Koopman eigenfunction exists a.e. in I.*

Proof The mapping, $t = \xi(\boldsymbol{x})$, is in C^1 a.e. in $\mathcal{X}$ since $\boldsymbol{x}(t)$ is in C^1 a.e. in I. Given that mapping, we define the following function:

$$\varphi(\boldsymbol{x}) = e^{\alpha\xi(\boldsymbol{x})+\beta}. \tag{4.5}$$

This function is in C^1 a.e. in $\mathcal{X}$. The time derivative of this function is

$$\frac{d}{dt}\varphi(\boldsymbol{x}(t)) = \frac{d}{d\xi}e^{\alpha\cdot\xi(x)+\beta}\nabla\xi(\boldsymbol{x})^T\frac{d}{dt}\boldsymbol{x} = \alpha\varphi(\boldsymbol{x}(t))\nabla\xi(\boldsymbol{x})^T P(\boldsymbol{x}(t)). \tag{4.6}$$

According to Lemma 4.6, $\nabla\xi(\boldsymbol{x})^T P(\boldsymbol{x}(t)) = 1$ a.e. Thus, the function in Eq. (4.5) admits Eq. (2.4) for any value of β, where the corresponding eigenvalue is $\lambda = \alpha$. □

From a differential geometry perspective, as noted earlier, $\boldsymbol{x}(t)$ forms a curve where its tangential velocity is $P(\boldsymbol{x})$. The absence of an equilibrium point is equivalent to nonzero velocity. This type of parametric curve, where the velocity is always nonzero, is called *regular*. The Koopman eigenfunction does not exist for nonregular curves.

Theorem 4.8 (Sufficient condition for the existence of a Koopman eigenfunction) *Let the conditions of Lemma 4.2 hold and one of the entries of the vector $P(\boldsymbol{x}(t))$ be either positive or negative $\forall t \in I$. Then, Koopman eigenfunctions exist a.e. in the time interval I.*

Proof If one of the entries in $P(x(t))$ is either positive or negative for all $t \in I$, then this entry is monotone and therefore injective. Then, the curve $\mathcal{X}$ is simple and open (see Courant and John [2012], pages 45, 177, and 207). Therefore, the time state-space mapping, $\xi(\boldsymbol{x})$, exists. Following Lemma 4.7, Koopman eigenfunctions can be expressed by (4.5). □

The following simple example illustrates the connections between the equilibrium point, finite time dynamics, and time state-space mapping.

Example 4.9 (Finite time support) Let us consider the following dynamics:

$$\frac{d}{dt}x = -2x^{\frac{1}{2}}, \quad x(0) = 1. \tag{4.7}$$

The solution is

$$x(t) = \begin{cases} (1-t)^2 & t \in [0,1] \\ 0 & t > 1 \end{cases}. \tag{4.8}$$

For $I = [0,1]$, the time state-space mapping is

$$t(x) = 1 - \sqrt{x}, \quad I = [0,1], \tag{4.9}$$

and using (4.5) with $\alpha = 1, \beta = 0$, we can express a Koopman eigenfunction by

$$\varphi(x) = e^{1-\sqrt{x}}. \tag{4.10}$$

Now, let us repeat this example with a different time interval. Let $I = [0, 1.5]$, containing the extinction time $T_{ext} = 1$. Note that, first, the time mapping, Eq. (4.9), does not hold in the entire interval, and the eigenfunction φ does not admit $\frac{d}{dt}\varphi(x) = \varphi(x)$ since $\varphi(x)$ is a nonzero constant for $t \in [1, 1.5]$.

Viewing a KEF as a direct result of a time state-space mapping leads us to an intuitive interpretation to *Extended DMD* (EDMD) of Williams et al. (2015a); see Appendix A.

4.1.4 Reconstruction Conservation Laws from KEFs

Conservation laws may be related to the energy or the momentum of a system. However, these notions can have a much broader sense. In general, a conservation law is a state-space measurement, $g : \mathbb{R}^N \to \mathbb{R}$, that does not change over time, hence admitting

$$\frac{d}{dt}g(\boldsymbol{x}) = 0. \tag{4.11}$$

This measurement can be seen as a Koopman eigenfunction with an eigenvalue $\lambda = 0$. Thus, the common approach argues that conservation laws are related to the null part of the Koopman spectrum.

On the other hand, dynamic reconstruction is based on the nontrivial Koopman eigenfunctions. Data-driven algorithms to reveal the dynamic (governing laws) and the conservation laws, based on Koopman operator theory, have been studied by Rudy et al. (2017), Brunton et al. (2016), Schmidt and Lipson (2009), Kaiser et al. (2018), and Langley et al. (1981). Dynamic reconstruction and conservation laws (such as energy, momentum, etc.) are perhaps the most crucial tasks in dynamical system analysis in general, and in control systems in particular.

We propose an alternative view. As discussed earlier, the relevant KEFs to system reconstruction are indeed not in the null part of the Koopman spectrum. However, from our perspective, after recovering the dynamical system (the governing laws) via KEFs the conservation laws naturally emerge from these nontrivial KEFs.

Lemma 4.10 (Revealing conservation laws from KEFs) *Let $\varphi(\boldsymbol{x})$ be a nontrivial Koopman eigenfunction. Then the measurement*

$$g(\boldsymbol{x}) := \frac{\nabla\varphi(\boldsymbol{x})^T P(\boldsymbol{x})}{\varphi(\boldsymbol{x})} \tag{4.12}$$

is a conservation law, where $g(\boldsymbol{x}) = \lambda$.

Proof We consider the measurement $\ln(\varphi(x))$. By using Eq. (2.4), we can express the time derivative of this measurement as

$$\frac{d}{dt}\ln(\varphi(\boldsymbol{x})) = \frac{\lambda\varphi(\boldsymbol{x})}{\varphi(\boldsymbol{x})} = \lambda.$$

On the other hand, using the chain rule we get

$$\frac{d}{dt}\ln(\varphi(\boldsymbol{x})) = \frac{\frac{d}{dt}\varphi(\boldsymbol{x})}{\varphi(\boldsymbol{x})} = \frac{\nabla\varphi(\boldsymbol{x})^T\frac{d}{dt}\boldsymbol{x}}{\varphi(\boldsymbol{x})} = \frac{\nabla\varphi(\boldsymbol{x})^T P(\boldsymbol{x})}{\varphi(\boldsymbol{x})}.$$

Comparing the preceding terms yields

$$\frac{\nabla\varphi(\boldsymbol{x})^T P(\boldsymbol{x})}{\varphi(\boldsymbol{x})} = \lambda. \tag{4.13}$$

□

Corollary 4.11 (Conservation laws induced by a state-space time mapping) *If a KEF is formulated by using a state-space time mapping, namely $\lambda = 1$, then Eq. (4.13) coincides with Eq. (4.3). This can be seen by*

$$\begin{aligned}\frac{d}{dt}\ln(\varphi(\boldsymbol{x})) &= \frac{d}{dt}\ln\left(e^t\right) = \frac{d}{dt}t \\ &= \frac{d}{dt}\xi(\boldsymbol{x}) = \nabla\xi(\boldsymbol{x})^T\frac{d\boldsymbol{x}}{dt} = \nabla\xi(\boldsymbol{x})^T P(\boldsymbol{x}) = 1.\end{aligned} \tag{4.14}$$

We illustrate the preceding results by two examples.

Example 4.12 (Free Fall) Let $x_1(t)$ and $x_2(t)$ be the height and the velocity of a mass in a free fall, respectively. The dynamical system is

$$\frac{d}{dt}\begin{bmatrix} x_1 \\ x_2 \end{bmatrix} = \begin{bmatrix} x_2 \\ -g \end{bmatrix},$$

where the initial condition is $\begin{bmatrix} h & 0 \end{bmatrix}^T$. The solution is

$$\begin{bmatrix} x_1 \\ x_2 \end{bmatrix} = \begin{bmatrix} h - \frac{1}{2}gt^2 \\ -gt \end{bmatrix}.$$

The time state-space mappings are

$$\begin{bmatrix} t_1 \\ t_2 \end{bmatrix} = \begin{bmatrix} \sqrt{\frac{2(h-x_1)}{g}} \\ -\frac{x_2}{g} \end{bmatrix}.$$

The induced conservation laws, using Eq. (4.13), are as follows.

Conservation Law #1 From Eq. (4.14) the conservation law is

$$1 = \nabla\xi(\boldsymbol{x})^T P(\boldsymbol{x}).$$

Corresponding to the dynamical system in this example, one can substitute $\nabla\xi(\boldsymbol{x})$ and $P(\boldsymbol{x})$ with

$$\nabla\xi(\boldsymbol{x}) = \left[-\frac{1}{2\sqrt{\frac{2(h-x_1)}{g}}}\frac{2}{g}. \quad 0\right]^T, \quad P(\boldsymbol{x}) = \left[x_2 \quad -g\right]^T.$$

It yields

$$1 = -\frac{1}{2\sqrt{\frac{2(h-x_1)}{g}}}\frac{2}{g}\cdot x_2,$$

which is the energy conservation law,

$$gx_1 + \frac{1}{2}x_2^2 = hg.$$

Conservation Law #2

$$\frac{d}{dx_2}t_2(x_2)\cdot\frac{d}{dt}x_2 = -\frac{1}{g}\cdot(-g) = 1$$

This conservation law is due to the constant acceleration g.

Example 4.13 (Pure rolling down an incline) On an inclined plane with a slope of angle α, a solid cylinder with mass m, radius R, and rotational inertia I_{cm} is released from rest. The location along the plane is denoted by x_1 and its velocity by x_2. The dynamical system is

$$\frac{d}{dt}\begin{bmatrix} x_1 \\ x_2 \end{bmatrix} = \begin{bmatrix} x_2 \\ \frac{g sin\alpha}{1+\frac{I_{cm}}{mR^2}} \end{bmatrix}, \tag{4.15}$$

with the initial condition $\boldsymbol{x} = [0,0]^T$. The solution is

$$\begin{aligned} x_1(t) &= \frac{1}{2}\frac{g sin\alpha}{1+\frac{I_{cm}}{mR^2}}t^2, \\ x_2(t) &= \frac{g sin\alpha}{1+\frac{I_{cm}}{mR^2}}t. \end{aligned} \tag{4.16}$$

The time mappings are

$$\begin{aligned} t_1(x_1) &= \sqrt{2\frac{1+\frac{I_{cm}}{mR^2}}{g sin\alpha}x_1}, \\ t_2(x_2) &= \frac{1+\frac{I_{cm}}{mR^2}}{g sin\alpha}x_2. \end{aligned} \tag{4.17}$$

Conservation Law #1

$$1 = \frac{d}{dx_1}t_1(x_1)\frac{dx_1}{dt} = \sqrt{2\frac{1+\frac{I_{cm}}{mR^2}}{g sin\alpha}}\frac{1}{2\sqrt{x_1}}x_2 \tag{4.18}$$

We can reformulate it as

$$\underbrace{\frac{1}{2}mx_2^2}_{E_K} + \underbrace{\frac{1}{2}I_{cm}\left(\frac{x_2}{R}\right)^2}_{E_R} \underbrace{-mgx_1 sin\alpha}_{E_P} = 0 \tag{4.19}$$

getting, as expected, that the sum of the energies (Kinetic, Rotational, and Potential) is zero.

Conservation Law #2 In the same manner as in Example 4.12, conservation law #2 is a result of constant acceleration.

4.2 Koopman Family

The KEF is of the form $\varphi(t) = e^{\alpha t+\beta}$, Eq. (4.5). This form of solution is unique, following standard ODE theory. However, this form is not unique in the sense of the time mapping (Eq. (4.5)). In this section, we leverage the multiplicity of KEFs to draw insights related to the dynamics and to possible applications.

4.2.1 Koopman Family and Its Ancestors

The set of Koopman eigenfunctions of a certain dynamic is generally infinite. However, many of the KEFs differ only by a certain simple manipulation (such as multiplication by a constant). Here, we define criteria that distinguish between different groups of KEFs. This extends the identities presented in Bollt (2021). The following lemma demonstrates that any mathematical manipulation on a KEF that maintains the form of Eq. (4.5) generates a new KEF.

Lemma 4.14 (Multiplicities of Koopman eigenfunctions) *If φ_1, φ_2 are Koopman eigenfunctions with the corresponding eigenvalues λ_1, λ_2, then:*

1. *The function $a \cdot \varphi_1$, $a \in \mathbb{R}$ is an eigenfunction with eigenvalue λ_1.*
2. *The function $(\varphi_1)^\alpha$, $\alpha \in \mathbb{C}$ is an eigenfunction with eigenvalue $\alpha\lambda_1$.*
3. *For any $n, m \in \mathbb{R}$ the function $(\varphi_1)^n (\varphi_2)^m$ is an eigenfunction with eigenvalue $n\lambda_1 + m\lambda_2$.*
4. *The function $(\varphi_1)^{\frac{\lambda}{\lambda_1}} + (\varphi_2)^{\frac{\lambda}{\lambda_2}}$ is an eigenfunction with eigenvalue λ.*

Proof This can be shown by

1. Using the linearity of the Koopman operator.
2. Writing the time derivative of $(\varphi_1)^\alpha$ explicitly we get

$$\frac{d}{dt}\left[\varphi_1^\alpha\right] = \alpha(\varphi_1)^{\alpha-1}\lambda_1\varphi_1 = \alpha\lambda_1\varphi_1^\alpha. \tag{4.20}$$

3. Similarly,

$$\begin{aligned}\frac{d}{dt}\left[(\varphi_1)^n(\varphi_2)^m\right] &= (\varphi_2)^m n(\varphi_1)^{n-1}\lambda_1\varphi_1 + (\varphi_1)^n m(\varphi_2)^{m-1}\lambda_2\varphi_2 \\ &= (n\lambda_1 + m\lambda_2)(\varphi_1)^n(\varphi_2)^m.\end{aligned} \tag{4.21}$$

4. Finally,

$$\begin{aligned}\frac{d}{dt}\left[(\varphi_1)^{\frac{\lambda}{\lambda_1}} + (\varphi_2)^{\frac{\lambda}{\lambda_2}}\right] &= \frac{\lambda}{\lambda_1}(\varphi_1)^{\frac{\lambda}{\lambda_1}-1}\lambda_1\varphi_1 + \frac{\lambda}{\lambda_2}(\varphi_2)^{\frac{\lambda}{\lambda_2}-1}\lambda_2\varphi_2 \\ &= \lambda\left[(\varphi_1)^{\frac{\lambda}{\lambda_1}} + (\varphi_2)^{\frac{\lambda}{\lambda_2}}\right].\end{aligned} \tag{70}$$

□

Discussion The multiplicities presented in Lemma 4.14 are translation and scaling of the time variable. Case 1 in this Lemma is a translation of the time axis and the rest of the cases are scaling. To distinguish between eigenfunctions that are generated from other eigenfunctions and "new" independent ones, we introduce the concepts of *Koopman family* and its *ancestors*.

Definition 4.15 (Koopman family) Let $\{\varphi_i\}_{i=1}^n$ be a finite set of KEFs. Let $k_P(\{\varphi_i\}_{i=1}^n)$ be the infinite uncountable set of KEFs generated by the finite set, recursively, according to the four options stated in Lemma 4.14. Let us define $k_P^m(\{\varphi_i\}_{i=1}^n) = k_P(k_P^{m-1}(\{\varphi_i\}_i^n))$. We term $\mathcal{K}_P(\{\varphi_i\}_i^n) = \cup_{m=1}^{\infty} k_P^m(\{\varphi_i\}_{i=1}^n)$ as the Koopman family of $\{\varphi_i\}_{i=1}^n$.

Definition 4.16 (Ancestors of a Koopman family) Let $\{\varphi_i^*\}_{i=1}^m$ be a finite set of KEFs. This set is an ancestor set of the Koopman family $\mathcal{K}_P(\{\varphi_i\}_{i=1}^n)$ if the following conditions hold:

1. $\varphi \in \mathcal{K}_P(\{\varphi_i\}_i^n) \Longleftrightarrow \varphi \in \mathcal{K}_P(\{\varphi_i^*\}_i^m)$.
2. $\varphi_j^* \notin \mathcal{K}_P(\{\varphi_i^*\}_{i=1, i\neq j}^m)$ for any $j = 1, 2, \cdots, m$.

Note that the subscript P is for the dynamical system, m is the number of elements in the ancestor set, and n is the number of elements in an arbitrary set of KEFs.

4.2.2 Koopman Eigenfunction Vector

A vector of Koopman eigenfunctions is denoted by

$$\boldsymbol{\varphi}(\boldsymbol{x}) = \begin{bmatrix}\varphi_1(\boldsymbol{x}) & \cdots & \varphi_L(\boldsymbol{x})\end{bmatrix}^T, \tag{4.23}$$

where L can be finite or infinite. The Jacobian matrix of this vector is

$$\frac{\partial}{\partial \boldsymbol{x}}\boldsymbol{\varphi}(\boldsymbol{x}) = \begin{bmatrix} \nabla\varphi_1(\boldsymbol{x})^T \\ \vdots \\ \nabla\varphi_L(\boldsymbol{x})^T \end{bmatrix} = \mathcal{J}(\boldsymbol{\varphi}). \tag{4.24}$$

Theorem 4.17 (Linear dynamic in Koopman family) *Let the conditions of Theorem 4.8 hold. The dynamical system, Eq. (2.1), P can be represented as a linear one with a vector of Koopman eigenfunctions, where the time derivative of this vector is*

$$\frac{d}{dt}\boldsymbol{\varphi}(\boldsymbol{x}) = \mathcal{J}(\boldsymbol{\varphi})P(\boldsymbol{x}) = \Lambda\boldsymbol{\varphi}(\boldsymbol{x}), \quad a.e. \tag{4.25}$$

where Λ is a diagonal matrix with the corresponding eigenvalues.

Proof We would like to show first the existence of an L-dimensional KEF. From Theorem 4.8 there exists a KEF. From Lemma 4.14, if there exists a KEF, there is an infinite set of KEFs, therefore, at least L eigenfunctions. According to the definition of the Koopman eigenfunction, the time derivative is

$$\begin{aligned}\frac{d}{dt}\boldsymbol{\varphi}(\boldsymbol{x}) &= \left[\tfrac{d}{dt}\varphi_1(\boldsymbol{x}), \cdots, \tfrac{d}{dt}\varphi_L(\boldsymbol{x})\right]^T \\ &= \left[\lambda_1\varphi_1(\boldsymbol{x}), \cdots, \lambda_L\varphi_L(\boldsymbol{x})\right]^T = \Lambda\boldsymbol{\varphi}(\boldsymbol{x}).\end{aligned} \tag{4.26}$$

On the other hand, applying the chain rule we get

$$\frac{d}{dt}\boldsymbol{\varphi}(\boldsymbol{x}) = \begin{bmatrix} \nabla\varphi_1(\boldsymbol{x})^T \\ \vdots \\ \nabla\varphi_L(\boldsymbol{x})^T \end{bmatrix} \frac{d}{dt}\boldsymbol{x}(t) = \mathcal{J}(\boldsymbol{\varphi})P(\boldsymbol{x}). \tag{4.27}$$

Note that $\varphi_i(\boldsymbol{x}) \in C^1$, *a.e.*, so the preceding expressions are valid only almost everywhere. □

The multiplicity of Koopman eigenfunctions results from either arithmetical manipulations (Def. 4.15) or the existence of several time state-space mappings (Def. 4.5). The main difference is the rank of the Jacobian, $\mathcal{J}(\boldsymbol{\varphi})$. Given a vector of KEFs, adding another Koopman eigenfunction from the Koopman family of the KEFs in the vector does not increase the rank of the Jacobian. However, adding a Koopman eigenfunction from another time state-space mapping does.

Lemma 4.18 (KEF gradients of a family) *Let $\mathcal{K}_P(\{\varphi_i^*\}_{i=1}^m)$ be the Koopman family of an ancestor set, $\{\varphi_i^*\}_{i=1}^m$. Let φ be a KEF in $\mathcal{K}_P(\{\varphi_i^*\}_{i=1}^m)$. Then, the gradient of φ, $\nabla\varphi$, is a linear combination of the gradients of the ancestor set for any $t \in I$.*

Proof Let $\mathcal{KG}$ be the linear span, defined by

$$\mathcal{KG} = span\left(\{\nabla\varphi_i^*\}_{i=1}^m\right) = \left\{\sum_{i=1}^m a_i\nabla\varphi_i^*,\ \forall a_i \in \mathbb{C}\right\}. \tag{4.28}$$

Let φ be in $\mathcal{K}_P(\{\varphi_i^*\}_{i=1}^m)$. According to Definition 4.15, there exist recursive steps leading from the ancestors $\{\varphi_i^*\}_{i=1}^m$ to φ. Now, by induction we show that $\nabla\varphi \in \mathcal{KG}$. Let us assume that from the ancestors to φ there is one step. Namely, φ is generated using φ_i^*, φ_j^*, according to the four cases of Lemma 4.14. The gradient of φ is a linear combination of the gradients of φ_i^* and φ_j^*. For cases 1, 2, and 4, the linearity is straightforward. For case 3, $\varphi = (\varphi_i^*)^n(\varphi_j^*)^l$, we have

$$\begin{aligned}\nabla\varphi &= \nabla(\varphi_i^*)^n\left(\varphi_j^*\right)^l = n\left(\varphi_i^*\right)^{n-1}\left(\varphi_j^*\right)^l\nabla(\varphi_i^*) + l\left(\varphi_i^*\right)^n\left(\varphi_j^*\right)^{l-1}\nabla\left(\varphi_j^*\right)\\ &= \left[\nabla\left(\varphi_i^*\right) \quad \nabla\left(\varphi_j^*\right)\right]\begin{bmatrix} n\left(\varphi_i^*\right)^{n-1}(\varphi_j^*)^l \\ l\left(\varphi_i^*\right)^n(\varphi_j^*)^{l-1}\end{bmatrix}.\end{aligned} \tag{4.29}$$

For any $t \in I$, the vector $\left[n\left(\varphi_i^*\right)^{n-1}(\varphi_j^*)^l \quad l\left(\varphi_i^*\right)^n(\varphi_j^*)^{l-1}\right]^T$ is constant. Therefore, the gradient of φ is in $\mathcal{KG}$. Now, we assume there exist k steps from the ancestors to φ. Let φ_i and φ_j be generated by $k-1$ steps. The induction assumption holds, meaning that their gradients are in $\mathcal{KG}$. Now, there is one step from φ_i and φ_j to φ. As shown, $\nabla\varphi$ is a linear combination of the gradients of its generators, $\nabla\varphi_i, \nabla\varphi_j$. But these vectors belong to $\mathcal{KG}$ by the induction assumption. Therefore, $\nabla\varphi \in \mathcal{KG}$. □

Remark 4.19 (Multiplicity of Koopman eigenfunctions) As noted in Bollt (2021), the algebraic multiplicity (Lemma 4.14) is not the only existing multiplicity. One can also perform manipulations on the time mapping $t(\boldsymbol{x})$. In this sense, the multiplicity of Koopman eigenfunctions is based on all functions f over the time mappings $\{t_i(\boldsymbol{x})\}$ that retain the time "physical unit." For example, if there are two time mappings $t_1(\boldsymbol{x})$ and $t_2(\boldsymbol{x})$, then $f(t_1, t_2) = \sqrt{t_1(\boldsymbol{x})t_2(\boldsymbol{x})}$ also is a time mapping and therefore e^f is also a KEF. In the general case, the minimal set $\{t_i(\boldsymbol{x})\}$ of time mappings for which the set $\{\nabla t_i(\boldsymbol{x})\}$ is independent is sufficient to span the entire domain of Koopman eigenfunctions.

4.2.3 Dynamics Reconstruction, Observability, and Controllability

The Jacobian matrix rank is related to system controllability and observability (see, for example, Brunton and Kutz (2019); Evangelisti (2011)). In the following, we formulate the connections between the rank of the Jacobian matrix, the size of the ancestor set, and time state-space mappings.

Dynamics Reconstruction

Proposition 4.20 (Sufficient condition for system reconstruction) *Consider the dynamical system* (2.1) *where* $x \in \mathbb{R}^N$. *Let us denote the Koopman family of all Koopman eigenfunctions of the dynamics as* $\mathcal{K}_P$. *An ancestor set of* $\mathcal{K}_P$ *is denoted as* $\{\varphi_i^*\}_{i=1}^n$. *The system can be reconstructed if* $N \le n$.

Proof According to Lemma 4.17, for any vector of KEFs the following equation holds:

$$\mathcal{J}(\varphi)P(x) = \Lambda\varphi(x), \quad (a.e.). \tag{4.30}$$

Let us choose a vector of ancestors, that is,

$$\varphi^*(x) = \begin{bmatrix}\varphi_1^*(x) & \cdots & \varphi_n^*(x)\end{bmatrix}^T. \tag{4.31}$$

According to Lemma 4.18, the rank of the Jacobian matrix is full and equal to N. Since the matrix $\mathcal{J}(\varphi)^T\mathcal{J}(\varphi)$ is invertible, the dynamics, P, can be revealed according to the following relation:

$$P(x) = \left(\mathcal{J}(\varphi)^T\mathcal{J}(\varphi)\right)^{-1}\mathcal{J}(\varphi)^T\Lambda\varphi(x), \quad (a.e.). \tag{4.32}$$

That is, we use the Moore–Penrose pseudo-inverse. □

Remark 4.21 (Sufficient condition for dynamic reconstruction) If each of the entries of P is either positive or negative for all t in I, then each entry of the state-space is monotone (and injective). We can formulate N different time state-space mappings from $\mathcal{X}$ to I (Theorem 4.8). These mappings induce N different KEFs. Therefore, the Jacobian matrix, $\mathcal{J}(\varphi)$, is $N \times N$ and full rank, therefore – invertible. Using Theorem 4.17, we can reconstruct the dynamics by

$$P(x) = \mathcal{J}^{-1}(\varphi)\Lambda\varphi(x). \tag{4.33}$$

Remark 4.22 (Reconstructing the dynamic – limitations) The recovery of the system, as described by Eqs. (4.32) and (4.33), is valid for a given initial condition x_0. In order to obtain a full recovery of the system, the properties of the initial condition should be taken into account.

Observability One can describe observability as the ability to recover the state of the system from measurements. A formal definition is as follows (Kou et al. [1973]).

Definition 4.23 (Observability) Let the dynamical system be

$$\begin{aligned} \frac{d\boldsymbol{x}}{dt} &= P(\boldsymbol{x}), \quad \boldsymbol{x}(t=0) = \boldsymbol{x}_0 \\ y &= h(\boldsymbol{x}), \end{aligned} \tag{4.34}$$

where $h\colon \mathbb{R}^N \to \mathbb{R}^M$ and $\boldsymbol{x}_0 \in Q_0 \subset \mathbb{R}^N$. This system is said to be completely observable in Q_0 if there exists a one-to-one correspondence between the set Q_0 of initial states and the set of trajectories of the observed output $\boldsymbol{y}(t)$.

Usually, the criteria of observability are based on the measurements, $h(\cdot)$ (Eq. (4.34)), and the time derivatives (whether they are injective or not). In the context of the Koopman theory, we can assess the observability differently. We examine the ability to recover the state-space trajectory by knowing only the initial condition and the Koopman eigenfunctions, where KEFs play the role of the measurements $h(\cdot)$.

Definition 4.24 (Observability in the context of Koopman theory) Consider the dynamical system Eq. (2.1). The system is fully observable if the state-space can be revealed from the KEFs and the initial condition.

Proposition 4.25 (Sufficient condition to observability) *Given the initial condition $\boldsymbol{x}_0$, if the system can be reconstructed it is observable in the sense of Def. 4.24.*

Proof The state-space can now be calculated as

$$\boldsymbol{x}(t) = \boldsymbol{x}_0 + \int_a^t P(\boldsymbol{x}(\tau))d\tau, \tag{4.35}$$

where $P(\cdot)$ is the reconstructed system from either Eq. (4.32) or (4.33). □

Controllability Controllability is a measurement for the ability to "move" the system from one state to another state. More formally, the general definition of controllability is formulated as follows; see Balakrishnan (1966).

Definition 4.26 (Controllability) Given a dynamical system

$$\frac{d\boldsymbol{x}}{dt} = P(\boldsymbol{x}) + u(t),$$

where $P(\cdot)$ is a nonlinear operator and $u(\cdot)$ is the input (time dependent). This system is *completely state controllable* if, for any initial condition $\boldsymbol{x}_1$, it is possible to find an input $u(t)$ such that the system reaches any other state $\boldsymbol{x}_2$ in finite time.

Remark 4.27 (Global controllability) Reconstructing the dynamical system enables us to enlarge the *Region of Attraction* (ROA), Eq. (2.45). Given the nonlinear dynamics,

$$\frac{d}{dt}\boldsymbol{x}(t) = P(\boldsymbol{x}(t)) + \boldsymbol{u}, \tag{4.36}$$

we can cancel the nonlinearity with the ancestors of a Koopman family $\varphi(\boldsymbol{x})$ if the dynamics is fully observable. In order to reach a stable system for any point $\boldsymbol{x}$ we define the following input $\boldsymbol{u}$,

$$\boldsymbol{u} = -\mathcal{J}^{-1}(\varphi)\Lambda\varphi(\boldsymbol{x}) + \boldsymbol{w}, \tag{4.37}$$

where the first element cancels the nonlinearity of the system (Remark 4.21) and the second term brings the system to any desired point in $\mathbb{R}^N$. Note that we assume there are no singular points in P.

4.3 Koopman Mode Decomposition

In the previous section, we have formulated KEFs using state-space time mappings. We would like now to show the relations of KMD to these functions. We examine the limitations of DMD to simulate the dynamical system. In addition, we show a direct relation between Koopman modes, Koopman eigenfunctions, and the dynamic. Finally, we note that the absence of explicit state-space time mapping does not necessarily indicate the inexistence of KMD.

The *Koopman Mode Decomposition* leverages the infinite set of a Koopman family (Definition 4.15) to reconstruct the observations from the Koopman eigenfunctions (Mezić [2005]). The reconstruction is a linear combination of Koopman eigenfunctions. For instance, the ith entry of $\boldsymbol{x}$ is assumed to be reconstructed as (Brunton et al. [2021])

$$x_i(t) = \sum_{j=1}^{\infty} v_{i,j}\varphi_j(\boldsymbol{x}(t)), \tag{4.38}$$

where $v_{i,j}$ is a scalar. Then, the state-space can be written as

$$\boldsymbol{x}(t) = \sum_{j=1}^{\infty} \boldsymbol{v}_j\varphi_j(\boldsymbol{x}(t)), \tag{4.39}$$

where $\boldsymbol{v}_j$ is an N-dimensional vector whose entries are the coefficients of the jth Koopman eigenfunction, namely $\boldsymbol{v}_j = \begin{bmatrix} v_{1,j} & \cdots & v_{N,j} \end{bmatrix}^T$. Substituting $\varphi(\boldsymbol{x})$ by Eq. (2.5), we get

$$\boldsymbol{x}(t) = \sum_{j=1}^{\infty} \boldsymbol{v}_j\varphi_j(\boldsymbol{x}(a))e^{\lambda_j t}. \tag{4.40}$$

The infinite triplet $\{\boldsymbol{v}_j, \varphi_j, \lambda_j\}_{j=1}^{\infty}$ is the Koopman mode decomposition, where $\{\boldsymbol{v}_j\}_{j=1}^{\infty}$ are the Koopman modes, $\{\varphi_j\}_{j=1}^{\infty}$ are the KEFs, and $\{\lambda_j\}_{j=1}^{\infty}$ are the Koopman eigenvalues. Note that the maximal index argument in the sum of (4.39) or (4.40) is not necessarily infinity. For example, it is enough to have one mode to reconstruct the linear dynamics initiated with one of its eigenvectors. In matrix notations, let V be a matrix whose column vectors are the corresponding Koopman modes. The state-space can be expressed as

$$\boldsymbol{x}(t) = V\boldsymbol{\varphi}(\boldsymbol{x}(t)). \tag{4.41}$$

Thus, the dynamical system has a linear representation with the measurements $\{\varphi_j(\boldsymbol{x})\}_{j=1}^{\infty}$; see Kaiser et al. (2021).

Example 4.28 (KMD of Zero-Homogeneous Dynamics) Let us consider the following dynamical system:

$$\frac{d}{dt}\boldsymbol{x} = P(\boldsymbol{x}), \quad \boldsymbol{x}(t=0) = \boldsymbol{v},\, t \in I = [0, -1/\lambda), \tag{4.42}$$

where P is a zero-homogeneous operator (admitting $P(a\cdot\boldsymbol{x}) = sign(a)P(\boldsymbol{x})$, $\forall a \in \mathbb{R}$), and $\boldsymbol{v}$ and λ are a nonlinear eigenvector and the corresponding eigenvalue of P, respectively (i.e. they admit the nonlinear eigenvalue problem $P(\boldsymbol{v}) = \lambda\boldsymbol{v}$). We assume a stable system, where $\lambda < 0$. More background on such problems is presented in Gilboa (2018). Then, the solution of the ODE is

$$\boldsymbol{x}(t) = \boldsymbol{v}\,(1 + \lambda t), \quad t \in I. \tag{4.43}$$

Let us recall that a KEF satisfies Eq. (2.4) and therefore can be formulated by the time state-space mapping as

$$\varphi(t) = e^t = e^{\frac{\frac{\langle \boldsymbol{x},\boldsymbol{v}\rangle}{\|\boldsymbol{v}\|^2}-1}{\lambda}}. \tag{4.44}$$

We would like now to express the solution (4.43) with Koopman eigenfunctions. To express the function t we have to apply the natural logarithm, ln, on the Koopman eigenfunction. Using Taylor series one can express it as

$$t = \ln(\varphi(\boldsymbol{x})) = \sum_{n=1}^{\infty}(-1)^{n+1}\frac{(\varphi(\boldsymbol{x})-1)^n}{n}. \tag{4.45}$$

Then, the solution of (4.43) can be written as

$$\boldsymbol{x}(t) = \boldsymbol{v}\left(1 + \lambda\sum_{n=1}^{\infty}(-1)^{n+1}\frac{(\varphi(\boldsymbol{x})-1)^n}{n}\right). \tag{4.46}$$

By expanding the terms $(\varphi - 1)^n$ we get an infinite polynomial with respect to the KEF φ. KMD emerges naturally.

4.3.1 Discussion

According to this example, since there is only one mode and its decay profile is not exponential, there can be many KEFs for one Koopman mode. The multiplicity of eigenvalues for one mode is related to the limitations of DMD. Since DMD recovers only linear dynamics, it cannot handle well one eigenvector with multiple eigenvalues.

We can now formulate the relation between Koopman modes and the dynamical system.

Proposition 4.29 (The Jacobian and Koopman modes) *Let $\boldsymbol{\varphi}(\boldsymbol{x})$ be a vector of Koopman eigenfunctions and $\mathcal{J}(\boldsymbol{\varphi}(\boldsymbol{x}))$ be its Jacobian matrix. In addition, let V be defined as in* (4.41). *Then, $P(\boldsymbol{x})$ is a right eigenvector of the matrix $V \cdot \mathcal{J}(\boldsymbol{\varphi}(\boldsymbol{x}))$ with eigenvalue one.*

Proof The time derivative of Eq. (4.41) is given by

$$\begin{aligned} &\frac{d}{dt}\boldsymbol{x} = V\frac{d}{dt}\boldsymbol{\varphi}(\boldsymbol{x}) \\ &P(\boldsymbol{x}) = V\mathcal{J}(\boldsymbol{\varphi}(\boldsymbol{x}))P(\boldsymbol{x}). \end{aligned} \tag{4.47}$$

□

Example 4.30 (Nonlinear system) Given the following system,

$$\frac{d}{dt}\begin{bmatrix} x_1 \\ x_2 \end{bmatrix} = \begin{bmatrix} x_1 \\ x_2 - x_1^2 \end{bmatrix}, \quad \begin{bmatrix} x_1(0) \\ x_2(0) \end{bmatrix} = \begin{bmatrix} 1 \\ 1 \end{bmatrix}, \tag{4.48}$$

the solution is

$$\begin{bmatrix} x_1 \\ x_2 \end{bmatrix} = \begin{bmatrix} 1 & 0 \\ 2 & -1 \end{bmatrix}\begin{bmatrix} e^t \\ e^{2t} \end{bmatrix}. \tag{4.49}$$

The time state-space mappings are

$$\begin{aligned} &t = \ln(x_1), \\ &t = \frac{1}{2}\ln(2x_1 - x_2). \end{aligned} \tag{4.50}$$

By choosing $\alpha = 1, \beta = 0$, the Koopman eigenfunctions, following (4.5), are

$$\begin{aligned} &\varphi_1(\boldsymbol{x}) = x_1, \\ &\varphi_2(\boldsymbol{x}) = \sqrt{2x_1 - x_2}. \end{aligned} \tag{4.51}$$

The state-space, $\begin{bmatrix} x_1 & x_2 \end{bmatrix}^T$, can be reconstructed by these eigenfunctions as

$$\begin{bmatrix} x_1 \\ x_2 \end{bmatrix} = \begin{bmatrix} \varphi_1(\boldsymbol{x}) \\ 2\varphi_1(\boldsymbol{x}) - \varphi_2(\boldsymbol{x})^2 \end{bmatrix} = \begin{bmatrix} 1 & 0 \\ 2 & -1 \end{bmatrix}\begin{bmatrix} \varphi_1(\boldsymbol{x}) \\ \varphi_2(\boldsymbol{x})^2 \end{bmatrix} = V\boldsymbol{\varphi}(\boldsymbol{x}). \tag{4.52}$$

We observe there are two modes, $[1,2]^T$ and $[0,-1]^T$, which evolve linearly under the nonlinear system (4.48). In addition, one can easily conclude that $V\mathcal{J}(\varphi(\boldsymbol{x}))$ yields an identity matrix, since

$$\mathcal{J}(\varphi(\boldsymbol{x})) = \begin{bmatrix} \nabla^T \phi_1(\boldsymbol{x}) \\ \nabla^T \phi_2^2(\boldsymbol{x}) \end{bmatrix} = \begin{bmatrix} 1 & 0 \\ 2 & -1 \end{bmatrix}. \tag{4.53}$$

Hence, $P(\boldsymbol{x})$ is an eigenvector for any $\boldsymbol{x}$.

We have shown the relation between time state-space mapping and Koopman eigenfunctions. The following proposition states a limitation between the two notions.

Proposition 4.31 (Existence of Koopman eigenfunctions with no time state-space mapping) *The state-space mapping is not a necessary condition for the existence of Koopman eigenfunctions.*

Proof This can be shown by the following simple example. Let us consider the linear system

$$\frac{d}{dt}\boldsymbol{x} = A\boldsymbol{x}, \quad \boldsymbol{x}(t=0) = \boldsymbol{x}_0, \tag{4.54}$$

where A is an $N \times N$ matrix. For simplicity, we assume the eigenvalues of A, $\{\lambda_i\}_{i=1}^N$, are unique and the eigenvector set, $\{\boldsymbol{v}_i\}_{i=1}^N$, is orthonormal. Then, the solution of this system of equations can be written as

$$\boldsymbol{x}(t) = \sum_{i=1}^{N} b_i \boldsymbol{v}_i e^{\lambda_i t}, \tag{4.55}$$

where the vector $\boldsymbol{b} = \begin{bmatrix} b_1 & \cdots & b_N \end{bmatrix}^T$ is chosen according to the initial condition. To form the Koopman eigenfunctions and, correspondingly, the Koopman mode, one should formulate the time state-space mapping. For each eigenvector and eigenvalue of A there is a mapping, expressed as

$$t_i(x) = \frac{1}{\lambda_i} \ln\left(\frac{\boldsymbol{v}_i^T \boldsymbol{x}}{b_i}\right). \tag{4.56}$$

Thus, the Koopman eigenfunctions are

$$\varphi_i(\boldsymbol{x}) = e^{t_i(x)} = \left(\frac{\boldsymbol{v}_i^T \boldsymbol{x}}{b_i}\right)^{\frac{1}{\lambda_i}}. \tag{4.57}$$

This expression can be simplified by applying Def. 4.15, yielding the following system:

$$\frac{d}{dt}\begin{bmatrix} v_1^T x \\ \vdots \\ v_n^T x \end{bmatrix} = \begin{bmatrix} \lambda_1 & & \\ & \ddots & \\ & & \lambda_n \end{bmatrix} \begin{bmatrix} v_1^T x \\ \vdots \\ v_N^T x \end{bmatrix}. \tag{4.58}$$

Note that if the eigenvector, v_i, is complex, then the time state-space mapping, Eq. (4.56), does not exist since it is not well defined. In this case, to create a time state-space mapping, we have to choose one branch from the ln function. However, the Koopman eigenfunction, Eq. (4.57), has a unique value, since the exponent cancels the ambiguity of the ln function. It shows that a Koopman eigenfunction can exist in cases where the time state-space mapping does not. □

5 Koopman Theory for PDE

Let us generalize the preceding results to the continuous setting of Koopman theory, following Nakao and Mezić (2020). We consider the solution of Eq. (2.7), based on the following assumptions.

Assumption 5.1 (Proper Operator) The operator $\mathcal{P}(f(x))$ in Eq. (2.7) is proper.

Lemma 5.2 (Continuous u) *If the operator $\mathcal{P}$ in Eq.* (2.7) *admits Assumption 5.1, then the solution is continuous in t.*

This is quite standard in the theory of PDEs. Basically, letting $u(x,t)$ be the solution of Eq. (2.7), we can write a first-order Taylor expansion for the variable t as

$$u(\mathrm{x}, t + dt) = u(\mathrm{x}, t) + \mathcal{P}(u(\mathrm{x}, t)) \cdot dt + o(dt). \tag{5.1}$$

Since the value of $||\mathcal{P}(u(\mathrm{x}, t))||$ is finite, we get $|u(\mathrm{x}, t + dt) - u(\mathrm{x}, t)| \rightarrow 0$ as $dt \rightarrow 0$.

Assumption 5.3 (Fréchet Differentiability) The operator $\mathcal{P}$ is Fréchet differentiable a.e. in $\mathcal{H}$.

If $\mathcal{P}$ admits Assumption 5.3, then the solution $u(\mathrm{x}, t)$ is in C^1 a.e. with respect to t (see e.g. Venturi and Dektor [2021]).

Definition 5.4 (Time mapping) Let $u(x,t)$ be the solution of the dynamical system (2.7), where $t \in I$. Let $\Xi(u)$ (Ξ is capital ξ) be a functional mapping from the solution u to t, that is,

$$t = \Xi(u). \tag{5.2}$$

Lemma 5.5 (Differentiation of time mapping) *Let Assumptions 5.1 and 5.3 hold. If the time mapping,* $t = \Xi(u)$*, exists, then it admits the following:*

$$\langle \partial\Xi(u(\mathrm{x},t)), \mathcal{P}(u(\mathrm{x},t))\rangle = 1 \quad a.e. \ in \ t \in I, \tag{5.3}$$

where $\partial\Xi(u(\mathrm{x},t))$ *is the variational derivative of* $\Xi(u(\mathrm{x},t))$.

Proof The mapping $\Xi(u(\mathrm{x}))$ is in C^1 a.e. in $t \in I$, since $u(\mathrm{x},t) \in C^1$ *a.e.* with respect to t in I. Based on the Brezis chain rule, the time derivative of the mapping is,

$$\begin{aligned} 1 &= \frac{d}{dt}t = \frac{d}{dt}\Xi(u) = \langle \partial\Xi(u(\mathrm{x},t)), \frac{d}{dt}u(\mathrm{x},t)\rangle \\ &= \langle \partial\Xi(u(\mathrm{x},t)), \mathcal{P}(u(\mathrm{x},t))\rangle. \end{aligned} \tag{5.4}$$

And this expression is valid almost everywhere. □

Proposition 5.6 (Condition for the inexistence of a Koopman eigenfunctional) *If there is an equilibrium point in I, then a nontrivial Koopman eigenfunctional does not exist.*

Proof Let $t_0 \in I$ be an equilibrium point and $\phi(u(\mathrm{x},t))$ be a Koopman eigenfunctional. Then, $u(\mathrm{x},t) = const, \forall t \in [t_0, b]$. Therefore, Eq. (2.10) does not hold for nontrivial ϕ for any $\lambda \neq 0$. □

5.1 Remark on Dynamics with Finite Time Support

Remark 4.4 is valid also for dynamics of the form of Eq. (2.7). Namely, if there exists a time point, $T_{ext} \in I$, for which $\mathcal{P}(u(\mathrm{x},t)) = 0, \forall t > T_{ext}$, then there is no Koopman eigenfunctional for this dynamics.

Lemma 5.7 (Koopman eigenfunctionals induced by a time state-space mapping) *Let the Assumptions 5.1 and 5.3 hold and* $u(\mathrm{x},t)$ *be the solution of Eq. (2.7). If there exists a time mapping,* $t = \Xi(u)$*, then a Koopman eigenfunctional exists.*

Proof Given the mapping, $t = \Xi(u)$, we define the following functional:

$$\phi(u) = e^{\alpha\Xi(u)+\beta}. \tag{5.5}$$

The time derivative of this functional is

$$\begin{aligned}\frac{d}{dt}\phi(u(\mathrm{x},t)) &= \frac{d}{d\Xi}e^{\alpha\cdot\Xi(u(\mathrm{x},t))+\beta}\frac{d}{dt}\Xi(u(\mathrm{x},t))\\ &= \alpha\phi(u(\mathrm{x},t))\langle\partial\Xi(u(\mathrm{x},t)),\frac{d}{dt}u(\mathrm{x},t)\rangle\\ &= \alpha\phi(u(\mathrm{x},t))\langle\partial\Xi(u(\mathrm{x},t)),\mathcal{P}(u(\mathrm{x},t))\rangle.\end{aligned} \tag{5.6}$$

According to Lemma 5.5, $\langle\partial\Xi(u(\mathrm{x},t)),\mathcal{P}(u(\mathrm{x},t))\rangle = 1$ a.e. Thus, the function in Eq. (5.5) admits Eq. (2.11) for any value of β, where the corresponding eigenvalue is $\lambda = \alpha$. □

Theorem 5.8 (Sufficient condition for the existence of a Koopman eigenfunctional) *Let the Assumptions 5.1 and 5.3 hold, let $u(\mathrm{x},t)$ be the solution of Eq. (2.7), and let there be a real function $f: I \to L$, for which $u(f(t),t)$ is monotonic with respect to t. Then, Koopman eigenfunctionals exist in the time interval I.*

Proof Let us define the following monotonic function,

$$g(t) = \int_0^L u(\mathrm{x},t)\delta(\mathrm{x}-f(t))dx, \tag{5.7}$$

where δ is the Dirac delta. Then, the time mapping is

$$t = \Xi(u) = g^{-1}\left(\int_0^L u(\mathrm{x},t)\delta(\mathrm{x}-f(t))dx\right). \tag{5.8}$$

According to Lemma 5.7, there exits a eigenfunctional, which can be expressed by Eq. (5.5). □

The assumption on the monotonicity of $u(f(t),t)$ is very strong. However, in dissipating smooth flow this assumption can be acceptable.

6 Mode Decomposition Based on Time State-Space Mapping

6.1 Bridging between Nonlinear Spectral Decomposition and KMD

Let us recall the dynamical system and its suggested form of solution. We consider the following PDE,

$$u_t = P(u), \tag{6.1}$$

where P is a nonlinear operator, $u(t=0)=f$. The solution of this PDE is approximated as

$$u(\mathrm{x},t) \approx \sum_{i=1}^{m} X_i(\mathrm{x})T_i(t), \tag{6.2}$$

where $\{X_i(x)\}_{i=1}^m$ are the spatial structures and $\{T_i\}_{i=1}^m$ correspond to the weighted mixture of the structures over time. We would like to mention two principal PDEs for which this approximation is precise (reaches equality). The first one is linear diffusion and the second is TV-flow (see the studies on spectral TV of Gilboa [2014], Burger et al. [2016], Bungert et al. [2019b]). In both cases, the temporal term $T_i(t)$ are the typical decay profiles of the operator that is dictated by its homogeneity. Whereas the decay profile of linear diffusion is exponential, that of TV-flow is linear. This was generalized by Cohen and Gilboa (2018, 2020), where it was shown there is a smooth transition between exponential and linear decay for γ-homogeneous operators, $\gamma \in [0, 1)$; see Fig. 2.1. These profiles can be calculated by analyzing an evolution initiated with a single (nonlinear) eigenfunction f, admitting $P(f) = \lambda f$. In this case it is simple to check that the evolution is structure preserving. That is, the spatial structure of f is maintained and only its contrast changes throughout the evolution. We thus get a separation of variables and can deduce the time profile. It was shown in Bungert and Burger (2019) that the typical decay profile is also the asymptotic behavior of the dynamic (at a time point just before extinction).

In Gilboa (2014) and Burger et al. (2016) it was suggested to perform a decomposition of the signal f by identifying phase transitions of the piecewise linear dynamics of TV, or of gradient flows of one-homogeneous functionals in general. This was performed simply by taking the second time derivative of the flow, where the time-weighted expression $\phi(x, t) = tu_{tt}(x, t)$ was referred to as a spectral component, admitting a simple reconstruction formula, $f = \int_0^\infty \phi(t)dt$. In Gilboa (2014) it was shown that not only the initial condition but the entire solution $u(x, t)$ can be expressed as a weighted integration of the spectral components,

$$u(x, t) = \int_0^\infty H(t, \tau)\phi(x, \tau)d\tau,$$

where $H(t, \tau) = ((\tau - t)/\tau)^+$. Comparing $\phi(x, \tau)$ to X_i and $H(t, \tau)$ to $T_i(t)$, we get an expression similar to (6.2), in an integral form. In Burger et al. (2016) it was shown that for the discrete one-dimensional TV-flow the number of components is finite and we can express the solution u by a sum of weighted spectral components. One can expand the linear decay profile, Eq. (2.28), where $\gamma = 0$, to an infinite sum of Koopman eigenfunctions, as shown in Eq. (4.46). Hence we can observe that the nonlinear spectral components ϕ are actually Koopman modes! These relations and connections are planned to be further investigated in a future work.

When the evolution is TV-flow, the set $\{\phi\}$ is referred to as spectral TV decomposition. In Cohen and Gilboa (2020) the idea was generalized to nonlinear decompositions of γ-homogeneous flows, $\gamma \in [0, 1)$. The typical decay profile is a truncated polynomial with fractional degree for almost every value of γ (see Fig. 2.1). Thus, the decomposition was based on fractional calculus, which made this process less efficient numerically.

To bypass the use of fractional calculus, it was suggested to apply DMD on the gradient descent of the respective homogeneous functional. As discussed earlier, it was shown that recovering the dynamic with DMD yields an inherent error; see Cohen et al. (2021a). A time rescaling method was proposed to improve the DMD decomposition. It was shown theoretically that an evolution of a single eigenfunction is constructed accurately and for general signals improvement in the decomposition was achieved. However, a major problem of phase changes in the flow, due to extinction of modes, was not addressed. This is most inherent in flows based on zero-homogeneous operators, common in signal and image processing. Alternative recent methods were suggested to improve DMD; however, none of them tackles well phase transitions in the flow. These methods use machine learning principles in the design of advanced DMD algorithms, such as EDMD (Williams et al. [2016, 2015a,b]) and *Kernel DMD* (KDMD) (Kawahara [2016]). Several learning-based approaches suggested to build a data-driven dictionary to reconstruct the dynamics sparsely; see Bollt (2021), Li et al. (2017), Pan et al. (2021), and Rudy et al. (2017). These works focus on learning the spatial structures that approximate Koopman modes. In other words, these algorithms aim at finding measurements that evolve linearly under the dynamical system.

Since DMD is primarily investigated in the context of fluid dynamics, oscillatory flows are more common, and less attention was directed to smoothing or decaying flows, which are most common in image and signal processing. We thus aim at extending the Koopman tools to this type of process. System reconstruction based on finding spatial structures has some limitations, most notably for processes with finitely decaying modes, since the reconstruction of KEFs may be infinite-dimensional. The reconstruction of a KEF as a polynomial of the observation, as in Example 4.9, contains an infinite vector of measurements, which is highly intractable numerically.

Our approach is based on the assumption that the observed dynamic has a typical monotone decay profile within a given time interval. Thus, instead of focusing on measurements that decay exponentially, the focus of our algorithm is on finding spatial structures that decay according to a predefined family of profiles.

Let us recall the generalized spectra which was introduced by Katzir (2017) and Gilboa (2018). This work focused on a decomposition induced by the typical decay profile of the respective operator. The spatial structures are deduced from a dictionary containing an overcomplete set of decay profiles. More formally, we would like to approximate a nonlinear dynamic,

$$\frac{d\boldsymbol{x}}{dt} = P(\boldsymbol{x}), \tag{6.3}$$

using a typical decay profile, $a_\lambda(t)$, which is controlled by a single scalar parameter λ. Given the time sampling point set $\{t_i\}_0^M$ (not to be confused with time state-space mapping), we define the data matrix

$$X = \begin{bmatrix} x(t_0) & x(t_1) & \cdots & x(t_M) \end{bmatrix} \tag{6.4}$$

and the overcomplete dictionary,

$$\mathcal{D} = \begin{bmatrix} a_{\lambda_0}(t_0) & \cdots & a_{\lambda_0}(t_M) \\ & \vdots & \\ a_{\lambda_L}(t_0) & \cdots & a_{\lambda_L}(t_M) \end{bmatrix}, \tag{6.5}$$

where L is large enough. An atom of this dictionary is a row. For instance, for a dictionary of exponential time profiles we have $a_\lambda(t) = e^{-\lambda t}$, $\lambda > 0$. For a dictionary of linear time profiles which extinct at zero (typical for TV-flow) we set $a_\lambda(t) = (1-\lambda t)^+$. We would like to extract the main spatial structures of the data matrix X, based on the corresponding decay profiles. As in many dimensionality reduction techniques, we assume the dynamic can be well represented by a sparse linear combination of spatial structures. One can formulate this as the following optimization problem,

$$\min \arg_{\mathcal{V}}\{\|X - \mathcal{V}\mathcal{D}\|_{\mathcal{F}}\}, \quad s.t. \|\mathcal{V}\|_0 < r, \tag{6.6}$$

where the columns of $\mathcal{V}$ are the spatial structures and the number of nonzero structures does not exceed r. In the rest of this section we show that for the case of equality, $X = \mathcal{V}\mathcal{D}$, if the decay profile is monotone, then the spatial structures resulting from the general spectral decomposition are the Koopman modes of KMD.

6.2 Generalized Dynamic Mode Decomposition

6.2.1 Spatiotemporal Mode Decomposition Based on a Monotone Decay Profile

Let us assume the dynamics, Eq. (6.3), induces a known typical monotone profile, $a_{\lambda_i}(t)$, for different spatial structures, v_i, in the data. The profile varies according to the spatial structure and depends on a parameter λ_i. In addition, we assume that the solution can be approximated using the form of spatiotemporal mode decomposition where the temporal functions are the decay profile with different λ_i. Then, we can reformulate the solution as

$$\boldsymbol{x}(t) = \sum_{i=1}^{N} v_i \cdot a_{\lambda_i}(t) + e, \tag{6.7}$$

where e is a small error term.

Since the time profile $a_{\lambda_i}(t)$ has been assumed to be monotone, there exists an inverse function for each atom, denoted as

$$t = \xi(a_{\lambda_i}(t)). \tag{6.8}$$

In matrix formulation, for a discrete time setting, this can be written as

$$\boldsymbol{t} = \boldsymbol{\xi}(\mathcal{D}), \tag{6.9}$$

where $\boldsymbol{t} \in \mathbb{R}^{(L+1)\times M}$. It is assumed that there exists a (sparse) mode matrix V that can approximate the samples of the system X using the dictionary by

$$X = V\mathcal{D} + e, \tag{6.10}$$

where $X = \begin{bmatrix} \boldsymbol{x}_0 & \cdots & \boldsymbol{x}_M \end{bmatrix}$ and e is a small error term.

Dimensionality Reduction Following the assumption of DMD, we would like to obtain a sparse representation of modes. This problem has been thoroughly investigated and can be formulated as Mairal et al. (2014b),

$$\min_V \|X - V\mathcal{D}\|_{\mathcal{F}}^2, \quad s.t.\|V\|_0 \leq r, \tag{6.11}$$

where $\|V\|_0 < r$ indicates the requirement that only up to r columns in V are not zero. This problem is NP-hard, and the sparsity constraint is relaxed to solving the following minimization problem:

$$\min_V \|X - V\mathcal{D}\|_{\mathcal{F}}^2 + \lambda\|V\|_1. \tag{6.12}$$

The solution of (6.12) is the minimizer of the left term when the nonzero modes (columns of the matrix V) are with norm of λ at least (see algorithm 6, p. 153 in Mairal et al. [2014b]).

In general, there are several well-known algorithms to recover the modes when the dictionary is known; see Elad (2010). We note that our problem is somewhat more difficult than the common signal processing case, since the atoms in the dictionary are highly coherent (strongly correlated). Here, we apply the implementation from Mairal et al. (2014a) for the Lasso algorithm (Eq. (6.12)) with a fine-tuning postprocessing stage (Appendix B) to solve this problem. The output of this algorithm is $\hat{V}$ and $\hat{\mathcal{D}}$, where each column in the matrix $\hat{V}$ contains a mode and $\hat{\mathcal{D}}$ has the corresponding atoms, taken from the dictionary $\mathcal{D}$. The entire dynamics can be approximated as

Algorithm 1 Koopman Mode Approximation

1: **Inputs:**
Data sequence $\{\boldsymbol{x}_k\}_0^N$ and typical profile $a_\lambda(t)$
2: Find modes $\hat{V}$ and dictionary $\hat{\mathcal{D}}$ (for example, invoke Algorithm 2 in Appendix B).
3: Formulate the decay profiles with the modes $\hat{V}$ and the data X, Eq. (6.14).
4: Formulate the time state-space mapping, Eq. (6.15).
5: **Outputs:**
Extract KEFs from the observations by Eq. (6.16).

$$X \approx \hat{V}\hat{\mathcal{D}}, \tag{6.13}$$

where $\approx$ denotes equality in the sense of Eq. (6.12).

Approximation of Koopman Eigenfunctions Given the modes $\hat{V}$ and the data matrix X and assuming $\hat{V}^T\hat{V}$ is invertible, one can express the dictionary as

$$\hat{\mathcal{D}} \approx (\hat{V}^T\hat{V})^{-1}\hat{V}^T X. \tag{6.14}$$

This reconstruction of the dictionary is necessary to be in the argument of the time state-space mapping, Eqs. (6.8) and (6.9), as follows:

$$t = \xi(\hat{\mathcal{D}}) = \xi((\hat{V}^T\hat{V})^{-1}\hat{V}^T X). \tag{6.15}$$

Thus, we can express with the dynamic measurements an exponential function. According to Eq. (4.5), the KEFs are given by

$$\varphi(X) = e^{t(X)} = e^{\xi((\hat{V}^T\hat{V})^{-1}\hat{V}^T X)}. \tag{6.16}$$

We summarize this algorithm in Algorithm 1.

Relation between Spatiotemporal Mode Decomposition and Koopman Mode Decomposition The definition of KMD is to express the state-space vector as spatiotemporal mode decomposition where the temporal terms are exponential functions (KEFs). This can be done easily by extracting the time variable t from Eq. (6.16) as

$$t = \ln(\varphi(x)) \tag{6.17}$$

and plugging it into Eq. (6.7) to get

$$\boldsymbol{x}(t) \approx \sum_{i=1}^{N} \boldsymbol{v}_i \cdot a_{\lambda_i}(\ln(\varphi(x))). \tag{6.18}$$

Then, the typical decay profile $a_{\lambda_i}(t)$ can be expressed using a Taylor series (under sufficient smoothness conditions) and we get

$$\boldsymbol{x}(t) \approx \sum_{i=1}^{N} \boldsymbol{v}_i \cdot a_{\lambda_i}(\ln(\varphi(x))) = \sum_{i=1}^{N} \boldsymbol{v}_i \cdot \sum_{j=0}^{\infty} \beta_i^j \varphi^j(x), \tag{6.19}$$

where β_i^j is the coefficient of $\varphi^j(x)$ in the Taylor series of $a_{\lambda_i}(\ln(\varphi(x)))$. By variation of parameter, the KMD is obtained (see Example 4.28).

Note that the preceding presentation is only intended to show a possible algorithmic path that is implied by our analysis. We limit the scope of our discussion here and leave for future work important issues, such as spectrum and system reconstruction accuracy, dimensionality reduction, robustness to noise, and prediction capacity; for more details on these concepts, see Gavish and Donoho (2014) and Lu and Tartakovsky (2020).

7 Examples

In this section, we apply the theory to a few examples. We examine the following: system reconstruction, global controllability, mode decomposition based on a dictionary of monotone profiles, and finding eigenfunctionals in partial differential equations.

Example 7.1 (System Reconstruction and Global Controllability) This example is based on Mauroy et al. (2020) (p. 10). Given the system

$$\frac{d}{dt}x(t) = P(x) + u = x - x^3 + u, \tag{7.1}$$

we would like to obtain complete controllability (see Definition 4.26) via a Koopman eigenfunction according to Remark 4.27. Let us recall that this remark states one can enlarge the region of attraction only with a feedback based on KEFs. In practice, under some conditions, after the feedback we get a system that is globally stable. Note that there are three equilibrium points $-1, 0$, and 1 with ROAs: $\mathcal{RA}(-1) = (-\infty, 0)$, $\mathcal{RA}(0) = \{0\}$, and $\mathcal{RA}(1) = (0, \infty)$, respectively. Applying the time state-space mapping to the solution of Eq. (7.1) yields

$$t(x) = \ln\left(\frac{x}{\sqrt{1-x^2}}\right) + C. \tag{7.2}$$

According to Theorem 4.8, one of the Koopman eigenfunctions is

$$\varphi(x) = e^{t(x)} = \frac{x}{\sqrt{1-x^2}}. \tag{7.3}$$

We set the input u to

$$u = -\mathcal{J}(\varphi)^{-1}\varphi + w, \tag{7.4}$$

where w is the input after feedback linearization. The Jacobian matrix is simply the derivative of φ with respect to x,

$$\mathcal{J}(\varphi) = \left(1 - x^2\right)^{-\frac{3}{2}}, \tag{7.5}$$

yielding

$$u = -\mathcal{J}(\varphi)^{-1}\varphi + w = -\left(1 - x^2\right)^{\frac{3}{2}} \frac{x}{\sqrt{1 - x^2}} + w = -x(1 - x)^2 + w. \tag{7.6}$$

Substituting this input in the dynamical system, Eq. (7.1), we get the following,

$$\frac{d}{dt}x(t) = P(x) + u = x - x^3 + u = x - x^3 - x(1 - x)^2 + w = w. \tag{7.7}$$

After the feedback any point in $\mathbb{R}$ becomes a state of indifference, as the time derivative of x is zero at any point in $\mathbb{R}$. This system is linear and controllable.

Example 7.2 (*Total Variation* eigenfunctional) A very common PDE in image processing is the gradient descent flow with respect to the total-variation (TV) functional; see a thorough analysis of this flow in Bellettini et al. (2002). For smooth functions u, TV can be expressed as

$$J_{TV}(u(\mathrm{x})) = \langle |\nabla u(\mathrm{x})|, 1 \rangle. \tag{7.8}$$

The gradient descent flow for this nonsmooth convex functional is defined by

$$u_t = \mathcal{P} \in -\partial J_{TV}(u), \qquad u(t = 0) = u_0, \tag{7.9}$$

where $\partial J_{TV}(u)$ denotes the subdifferential of TV at u. The flow is known also as the 1-Laplacian flow. When $\mathrm{x} \in L \subset \mathbb{R}$ the solution is piecewise linear, at any time interval I_j the solution admits; see Cohen et al. (2021b):

$$u(\mathrm{x}, t) = h_{1,j}(\mathrm{x}) + h_{2,j}(\mathrm{x})\lambda_j t, \tag{7.10}$$

where $h_{1,j}, h_{2,j}$ are the modes evolved in the interval I_j. It was shown in Cohen et al. (2021b), following the analysis of Burger et al. (2016), that the two modes are orthogonal, $h_{1,j} \perp h_{2,j}$. Thus, at each interval there are two eigenfunctionals, as defined and characterized by (2.9), (2.10), and (2.11). The trivial one is an eigenfunctional with eigenvalue zero:

$$\phi_1(u) = \langle h_1, u \rangle. \tag{7.11}$$

The second one corresponds to the linearly evolving mode,

$$\phi_2(u) = e^t = e^{\frac{\langle h_{2,j}, u \rangle}{\|h_{2,j}\|^2 \lambda_j}}. \tag{7.12}$$

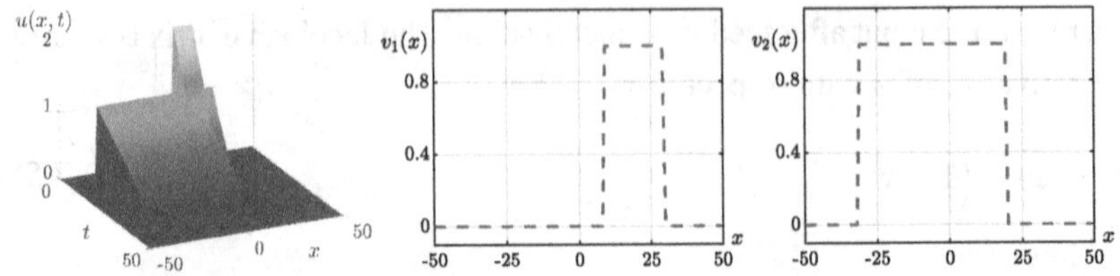

(a) $u(x, t)$ (b) v_1 (c) v_2

Figure 7.4 (a) The solution of Eq. (7.13). On the right are the spatial structures (modes), v_1 (b) and v_2 (c). They evolve with linear decay at a rate of $\lambda_1 = 1/10$ and $\lambda_2 = 1/30$, respectively.

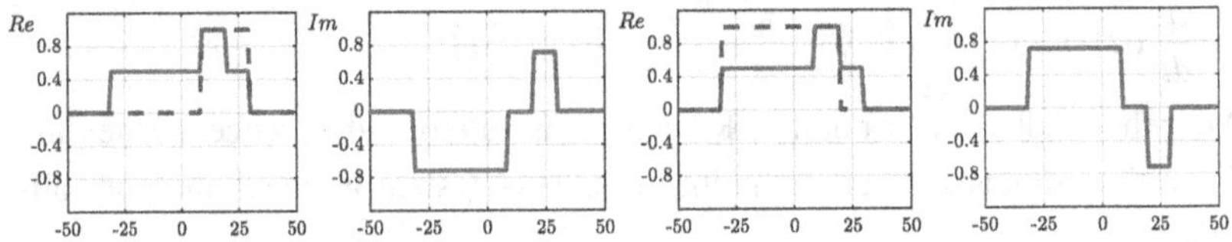

(a) Dynamic Mode Decomposition.Two plots on the left: real and imaginary values of the first DMD mode, compared to v_1 (dashed). Two plots on the right: real and imaginary values of the second DMD mode, compared to v_2 (dashed).

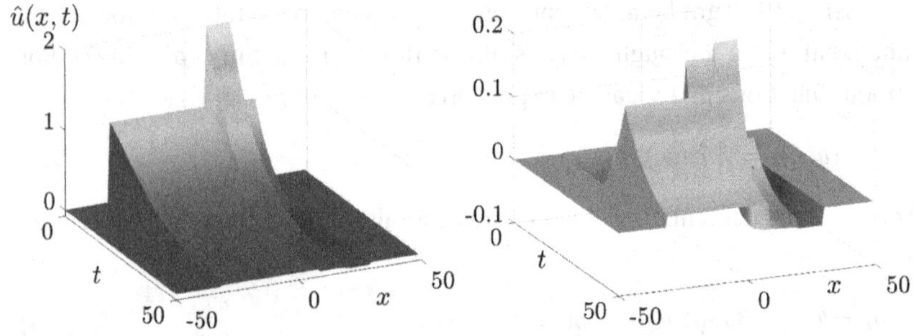

(b) Reconstruction (c) Error $u(x,t) - \hat{u}(x,t)$

Figure 7.5 Dynamic Mode Decomposition and Reconstruction. Top row: First two DMD modes, compared to v_i. Bottom row: Reconstruction through Eq. (2.13) (left) and the corresponding error (right). We can observe the dynamics is not reconstructed well and the error is significant.

Example 7.3 (Nonlinear PDE # 2) Let the solution of Eq. (2.7) be

$$u(\mathrm{x},t) = v_1(\mathrm{x}) \cdot a_1(t) + v_2(\mathrm{x}) \cdot a_2(t). \tag{7.13}$$

The solution $u(x,t)$ and the spatial structures $v_i(x)$, $i \in \{1,2\}$, are depicted in Fig. 7.4. The decay profile is of the form $a_i(t) = (1+\lambda_i t)^+$, where $\lambda_1 = 1/10$ and $\lambda_2 = 1/30$. DMD yields the decomposition depicted in Fig. 7.5. The modes are complex and each of them is depicted in two graphs, the real and the imaginary

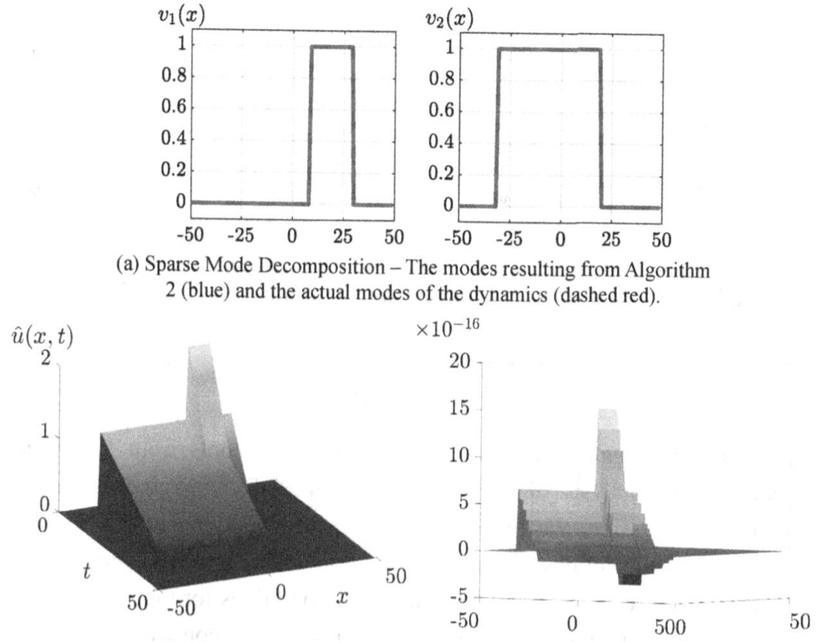

(a) Sparse Mode Decomposition – The modes resulting from Algorithm 2 (blue) and the actual modes of the dynamics (dashed red).

(b) **Reconstruction** (c) **Error** $u(x,t) - \hat{u}(x,t)$

Figure 7.6 Sparse Mode Decomposition and Reconstruction (Algorithm 2) – (a) Sparse mode decomposition compared to the modes, ν_1 and ν_2. (b) Dynamic reconstruction with Algorithm 2 (Eq. (6.13)) (c) The corresponding error. Correct modes are obtained, yielding close to perfect reconstruction of the dynamics.

parts (Fig. 7.5a). It demonstrates the limitations of DMD in systems with typical dynamics that are not exponential.

The decomposition resulting from Algorithm 2 is depicted in Fig. 7.6. The modes are shown in Fig. 7.6a and recover the modes accurately. The entire dynamics reconstruction is given in Fig. 7.6b with the corresponding error in Fig. 7.6c. Having the modes, we can find the eigenfunctionals:

$$\boldsymbol{\phi}(t) = \begin{bmatrix} \langle \nu_1, \nu_1 \rangle & \langle \nu_1, \nu_2 \rangle \\ \langle \nu_2, \nu_1 \rangle & \langle \nu_2, \nu_2 \rangle \end{bmatrix}^{-1} \begin{bmatrix} \langle \nu_1(\mathrm{x}), u(\mathrm{x}, t) \rangle \\ \langle \nu_2(\mathrm{x}), u(\mathrm{x}, t) \rangle \end{bmatrix} - \begin{bmatrix} 1 \\ 1 \end{bmatrix}. \tag{7.14}$$

They are depicted in Fig. 7.7. One can see that the eigenfunctionals are valid until the vanishing points. The first mode vanishes at $t = 10$ and the second at $t = 30$.

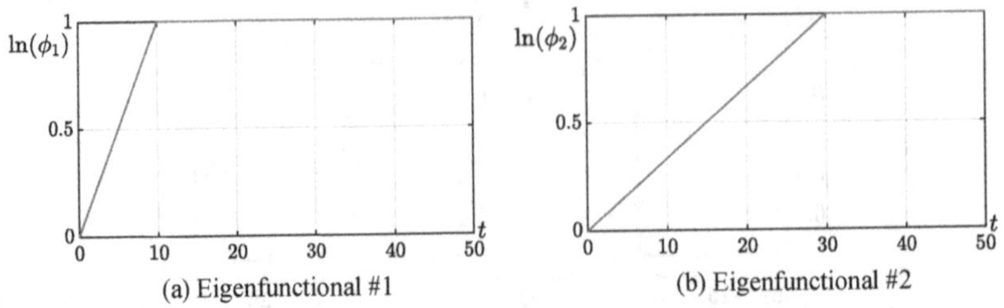

Figure 7.7 Eigenfunctionals – based on the monotone decay profile dictionary. These are the eigenfunctionals formulated in Eq. (7.14).

8 Conclusion

This work investigates ways to broaden the use of tools from Koopman theory for the analysis of local and nonlocal PDEs emerging in image and signal processing. We focus on evolution of smoothing processes with possible phase transitions in the dynamics, inherent in zero-homogeneous operators. We discuss necessary and sufficient conditions for the existence of Koopman eigenfunctions. We examine KMD, system reconstruction, global linearity, controllability, and observability through Koopman theory. These insights highlight some limitations of DMD. With the technique of time state-space mapping, we show how conservation laws emerge naturally from any KEF. In addition, we justify the approximation of EDMD based on this mapping.

The classical DMD accurately evaluates KMD as long as KEFs are linear combinations of the observations and KMD is finite-dimensional. However, DMD has clear limitations in four different settings: (1) the typical decay profile of the system is not exponential; (2) one Koopman mode is associated with multiple eigenvalues; (3) there is an equilibrium point in the time interval I; 4) Koopman modes do not exist for all t in I. Another limitation emerges when the dynamic P is in C^0 almost everywhere. In this case, some of the modes might vanish at different times, as we see in the total-variation flow.

We suggest a new type of decomposition to overcome these fundamental problems. It is based on inverse time state-space mapping of injective curves. We implement this method using overcomplete dictionaries of monotone profiles, typical to the dynamics. This decomposition coincides with a basic assumption of DMD – a flow can be sparsely represented by a few dominant modes. We show our decomposition yields Koopman modes. This work can lead to many interesting connections between decomposition, signal representation, nonlinear PDEs, and their relation to Koopman theory.

Symbols

$\boldsymbol{x}_i$	The ith sample of the state vector belongs to $\mathbb{R}^N$
X	Contains the samples of the dynamics $X = \begin{bmatrix} \boldsymbol{x}_0 & \cdots & \boldsymbol{x}_M \end{bmatrix}$ belongs to $\mathbb{R}^{N\times(M+1)}$
$\mathcal{U}$	A matrix where $\mathcal{U}_{i,j} = u(x_i, t_j)$
H	A auto-correlation matrix of the set $\{h_i\}_{i=1}^M$
$\boldsymbol{Hu}$	A vector where $\boldsymbol{Hu}_i = \langle h_i(x), u(x,t)\rangle$
$\boldsymbol{h}(x)$	A vector $\boldsymbol{h}_i(x) = h_i(x)$
$\mathcal{V}$	Contains the main spatial structures $\{\boldsymbol{v}_i\}$
$\mathcal{D}$	A dictionary of a family of a decay profile
P	A (nonlinear) function $P\colon \mathbb{R}^N \to \mathbb{R}^N$ in C^1 a.e.
t	Time index where $t \in \mathbb{R}^+$
g	This is an observation function of the state vector $\boldsymbol{x}$, $g\colon \mathbb{R}^N \to \mathbb{R}$
K_P^τ	The Koopman operator. The superscript denotes the time parameter and the subscript denotes the dynamical system
I	An interval $[a, b]$ in the time axis
$\varphi(\boldsymbol{x}(t))$	A Koopman eigenfunction
λ	A Koopman eigenvalue
∇	The gradient of a function
T	Denotes the transpose of a matrix
$\mathcal{H}$	A Hilbert space
$\mathcal{P}$	An (nonlinear) operator $\mathcal{P}\colon \mathcal{H} \to \mathcal{H}$
Q	A (nonlinear) proper, lower-semicontinuous functional $Q\colon \mathcal{H} \to \mathbb{R}$
$\phi(\cdot)$	A Koopman eigenfunctional
$\boldsymbol{v}_i$	A preserved spatial shape under the dynamics P
$h_i(x)$	A preserved spatial shape under the dynamics $\mathcal{P}$
$a_i(t)$	The time profile corresponding to the ith preserved spatial shape
$\gamma, \gamma - 1$	Denote the homogeneity degrees of a functional and its variational derivative, respectively
X_0^{M-1}, X_1^M	Data matrices $[\boldsymbol{x}_0, \cdots, \boldsymbol{x}_{M-1}], [\boldsymbol{x}_1, \cdots, \boldsymbol{x}_M]$

U, Σ, V	*Singular Value Decomposition* (SVD) of $\boldsymbol{x}_0^{N-1}$
U_r, V_r	Submatrices of U, V containing the first r columns
Σ_r	Submatrix of Σ containing the most significant r eigenvalues of the SVD that are the diagonal of Σ
$\mathcal{X}$	The curve in $\mathbb{R}^N$ representing the solution $\boldsymbol{x}$
$\xi(\cdot)$	A mapping from the curve $\boldsymbol{x}(t)$ to the time variable t
$\varphi(\boldsymbol{x})$	A Koopman mode
$\mathcal{J}(\varphi(\boldsymbol{x}))$	The Jacobian of Koopman mode $\varphi(\boldsymbol{x})$
Ξ	A functional mapping from $u(x,t)$ to t
ϕ	An eigenfunctional

Abbreviations

DMD	*Dynamic Mode Decomposition*
EDMD	*Extended DMD*
KDMD	*Kernel DMD*
KEF	*Koopman Eigenfunction*
KEFal	*Koopman Eigenfunctional*
KMD	*Koopman Mode Decomposition*
ODE	*Ordinary Differential Equation*
PDE	*Partial Differential Equation*
ROA	*Region of Attraction*
S-DMD	*Symmetric DMD*
SVD	*Singular Value Decomposition*
TV	*Total Variation*

Appendix A

Extended Dynamic Mode Decomposition Induced from Inverse Mapping

One of the methods to increase the accuracy of the classic *Dynamic Mode Decomposition* DMD is by enriching the state-space vector with nonlinear measurements of the coordinates $\boldsymbol{x}$; see Williams et al. (2015b). It is shown that this approach indeed improves accuracy. Here, we can interpret this approach as the Taylor expansion of Koopman eigenfunctions. This provides both justification and a clear method for supplying additional measurements. Let us expand the Koopman eigenfunction, $\varphi(\boldsymbol{x}) = e^{\xi(\boldsymbol{x})}$, by a Taylor series,

$$\varphi(\boldsymbol{x}) = e^{\xi(\boldsymbol{x})} = \sum_{j=0}^{\infty} \frac{\xi(\boldsymbol{x})^j}{j!}.$$

We can approximate this expression by taking only a finite number of elements from this sum:

$$e^{\xi(\boldsymbol{x})} \approx \sum_{j=0}^{M} \frac{\xi(\boldsymbol{x})^j}{j!}.$$

Thus, Eq. (2.4) can be approximated as

$$\frac{d}{dt}\sum_{j=0}^{M} \frac{\xi(\boldsymbol{x})^j}{j!} \approx \sum_{j=0}^{M-1} \frac{\xi(\boldsymbol{x})^j}{j!}. \tag{A.1}$$

In matrix notation, this approximation can be reformulated as

$$\frac{d}{dt}\begin{bmatrix} 1 \\ \xi(\boldsymbol{x}) \\ \vdots \\ \frac{\xi(\boldsymbol{x})^M}{M!} \end{bmatrix} \approx A \begin{bmatrix} 1 \\ \xi(\boldsymbol{x}) \\ \vdots \\ \frac{\xi(\boldsymbol{x})^M}{M!} \end{bmatrix}, \tag{A.2}$$

where any matrix A with a left-eigenvector $\begin{bmatrix} 1 & \cdots & 1 \end{bmatrix}$ can be an optional solution to Eq. (A.2) for which Eq. (A.1) holds. In addition, taking M to infinity, A gets the form

$$[A]_{i,j} = \begin{cases} 1 & i = j+1 \\ 0 & else \end{cases},$$

where $[A]_{i,j}$ is the i, jth entry of A.

Appendix B
Sparse Representation

The generalized dynamic mode decomposition, proposed in Section 6, is a sparse representation of the dynamics. It is assumed that the dynamic can be formulated as

$$X = V\mathcal{D} + e,$$

where $X = \begin{bmatrix} \boldsymbol{x}_0 & \cdots & \boldsymbol{x}_M \end{bmatrix}$, V contains the spatial modes, $\mathcal{D}$ contains an overcomplete set of the typical decay profiles, and e is a small error term. A common problem in sparse representation, in general, is when the atoms of the dictionary have a strong correlation; see Katzir (2017). In the following algorithm, we suggest a naive algorithm to remove the irrelevant modes. This algorithm is used as postprocessing of a sparse representation algorithm; see Mairal et al. (2014b).

Algorithm 2 Sparse Representation

1: **Inputs:**

    Data sequence $\{x_k\}_0^M$ and decay dictionary $\mathcal{D}$

2: **Initialize:**

    $\mathcal{SR} = \emptyset$

3: Find the sparse representation V according to Mairal et al. (2014a).

4: Let $\mathcal{I}$ be the set of indices of the atoms in $\mathcal{D}$ sorted (from low to high) according to the norm of the modes (column vectors of V).

5: Remove from $\mathcal{I}$ the indices for which the modes are zeros.

6: **while** True **do**

7:     Define $\hat{\mathcal{D}}$ as a new dictionary containing the atoms with indices $\mathcal{I}$.

8:     Compute $\hat{V} = X\hat{\mathcal{D}}^T(\hat{\mathcal{D}}\hat{\mathcal{D}}^T)^{-1}$

9:     Compute the error $\|X - \hat{V}\hat{\mathcal{D}}\|_{\mathcal{F}}^2$

10:     Add the set $\mathcal{I}$ and its corresponding error to $\mathcal{SR}$

11:     Remove the first index in $\mathcal{I}$.

12:     **if** $\mathcal{I}$ is empty **then**

13:         Break

14:     **end if**

15: **end while**

16: Find in $\mathcal{SR}$ the set of indices $\mathcal{I}$ that yields the minimum error

17: Define $\hat{\mathcal{D}}$ as a new dictionary containing the atoms with indices $\mathcal{I}$.

18: Compute $\hat{V} = X\hat{\mathcal{D}}^T(\hat{\mathcal{D}}\hat{\mathcal{D}}^T)^{-1}$

19: **Outputs:**

$$\hat{V}, \hat{\mathcal{D}}$$

References

Andreu, Fuensanta, Ballester, Coloma, Caselles, Vicent, and Mazón, José. 2001. Minimizing total variation flow. *Differential and Integral Equations*, **14**(3), 321–360.

Askham, Travis, and Kutz, J. Nathan. 2018. Variable projection methods for an optimized dynamic mode decomposition. *SIAM Journal on Applied Dynamical Systems*, **17**(1), 380–416.

Aubry, Nadine, Guyonnet, Régis, and Lima, Ricardo. 1991. Spatiotemporal analysis of complex signals: Theory and applications. *Journal of Statistical Physics*, **64**(3), 683–739.

Balakrishnan, Alampallam. 1966. On the controllability of a nonlinear system. *Proceedings of the National Academy of Sciences of the United States of America*, **55**(3), 465–468.

Bellettini, Giovanni, Caselles, Vicent, and Novaga, Matteo. 2002. The total variation flow in RN. *Journal of Differential Equations*, **184**(2), 475–525.

Bollt, Erik. 2021. Geometric considerations of a good dictionary for Koopman analysis of dynamical systems: Cardinality, "primary eigenfunction," and efficient representation. *Communications in Nonlinear Science and Numerical Simulation*, **100**, 105833.

Brezis, Haim. 1973. *Opérateurs maximaux monotones et semi-groupes de contractions dans les espaces de Hilbert*. Elsevier.

Brunton, Steven, Budišić, Marko, Kaiser, Eurika, and Kutz, J. Nathan. 2021. Modern Koopman theory for dynamical systems. *SIAM Review*, **64**(2), 229–340. *arXiv:2102.12086.*

Brunton, Steven, and Kutz, J. Nathan. 2019. *Data-Driven Science and Engineering: Machine Learning, Dynamical Systems, and Control*. Cambridge University Press.

Brunton, Steven, Proctor, Joshua, and Kutz, J. Nathan. 2016. Discovering governing equations from data by sparse identification of nonlinear dynamical systems. *Proceedings of the National Academy of Sciences*, **113**(15), 3932–3937.

Bungert, Leon, and Burger, Martin. 2019. Asymptotic profiles of nonlinear homogeneous evolution equations of gradient flow type. *Journal of*

Evolution Equations, **20**, 1061–1092.

Bungert, Leon, Burger, Martin, and Tenbrinck, Daniel. 2019a. Computing nonlinear eigenfunctions via gradient flow extinction. Pages 291–302 of *International Conference on Scale Space and Variational Methods in Computer Vision*. Lecture Notes in Computer Science book series, volume 11603. Springer. DOI: https://doi.org/10.1007/978-3-030-22368-7_23.

Bungert, Leon, Burger, Martin, Chambolle, Antonin, and Novaga, Matteo. 2019b. Nonlinear spectral decompositions by gradient flows of one-homogeneous functionals. *Analysis & PDE*, **14**(3), 823–860. *arXiv:1901.06979*.

Burger, Martin, Gilboa, Guy, Moeller, Michael, Eckardt, Lina, and Cremers, Daniel. 2016. Spectral decompositions using one-homogeneous functionals. *SIAM Journal on Imaging Sciences*, **9**(3), 1374–1408.

Chuaqui, Martin. 2018. General criteria for curves to be simple. *Journal of Mathematical Analysis and Applications*, **464**(1), 955–963.

Cohen, Ido, and Gilboa, Guy. 2018. Shape preserving flows and the p–Laplacian spectra. HAL Id: hal-01870019. https://hal.science/hal-01870019.

Cohen, Ido, and Gilboa, Guy. 2020. Introducing the p-Laplacian spectra. *Signal Processing*, **167**, 107281. DOI: https://doi.org/10.1016/j.sigpro.2019.107281 .

Cohen, Ido, Azencot, Omri, Lifshits, Pavel, and Gilboa, Guy. 2021a. Modes of homogeneous gradient flows. *SIAM Journal on Imaging Sciences*, **14**(3), 913–945.

Cohen, Ido, Berkov, Tom, and Gilboa, Guy. 2021b. Total-variation mode decomposition. Pages 52–64 of *Scale Space and Variational Methods in Computer Vision*, edited by Abderrahim Elmoataz, Jalal Fadili, Yvain Quéau, Julien Rabin, and Loïc Simon. Springer.

Cohen, Ido, Falik, Adi, and Gilboa, Guy. 2019. Stable explicit p-Laplacian flows based on nonlinear eigenvalue analysis. Pages 315–327 of *International Conference on Scale Space and Variational Methods in Computer Vision*, edited by Jan Lellmann, Jan Modersitzki, and Martin Burger. Lecture Notes in Computer Science, volume 11603. Springer.

Courant, Richard, and John, Fritz. 2012. *Introduction to Calculus and Analysis I*. Springer.

Dawson, Scott, Hemati, Maziar, Williams, Matthew, and Rowley, Clarence. 2016. Characterizing and correcting for the effect of sensor noise in the dynamic mode decomposition. *Experiments in Fluids*, **57**(3), 42. DOI: https://doi.org/10.1007/s00348-016-2127-7.

Elad, Michael. 2010. *Sparse and Redundant Representations: From Theory to Applications in Signal and Image Processing*. Springer.

Evangelisti, E. 2011. *Controllability and Observability: Lectures Given at a Summer School of the Centro Internazionale Matematico Estivo (CIME) held in Pontecchio (Bologna), Italy, July 1–9, 1968*. CIME Summer Schools, volume 46. Springer.

Gavish, Matan, and Donoho, David. 2014. The optimal hard threshold for singular values is $4/\sqrt{3}$. *IEEE Transactions on Information Theory*, **60**(8), 5040–5053.

Giannakis, Dimitrios. 2019. Data-driven spectral decomposition and forecasting of ergodic dynamical systems. *Applied and Computational Harmonic Analysis*, **47**(2), 338–396.

Giannakis, Dimitrios, and Majda, Andrew. 2012. Nonlinear Laplacian spectral analysis for time series with intermittency and low-frequency variability. *Proceedings of the National Academy of Sciences*, **109**(7), 2222–2227.

Gilboa, Guy. 2014. A total variation spectral framework for scale and texture analysis. *SIAM Journal on Imaging Sciences*, **7**(4), 1937–1961.

Gilboa, Guy. 2018. *Nonlinear Eigenproblems in Image Processing and Computer Vision*. Springer.

Gilboa, Guy, and Osher, Stanley. 2009. Nonlocal operators with applications to image processing. *Multiscale Modeling & Simulation*, **7**(3), 1005–1028.

Hemati, Maziar, Rowley, Clarence, Deem, Eric, and Cattafesta, Louis. 2017. De-biasing the dynamic mode decomposition for applied Koopman spectral analysis of noisy datasets. *Theoretical and Computational Fluid Dynamics*, **31**(4), 349–368.

Kaiser, Eurika, Kutz, J. Nathan, and Brunton, Steven. 2018. Discovering conservation laws from data for control. Pages 6415–6421 of *2018 IEEE Conference on Decision and Control (CDC)*. Institute of Electrical and Electronics Engineers.

Kaiser, Eurika, Kutz, J. Nathan, and Brunton, Steven. 2021. Data-driven discovery of Koopman eigenfunctions for control. *Machine Learning: Science and Technology*, **2**(3), 035023. DOI: https://doi.org/10.1088/2632-2153/abf0f5.

Katzir, Oren. 2017. On the scale-space of filters and their applications. M.Phil. thesis, Technion – Israel Institute of Technology, Haifa.

Kawahara, Yoshinobu. 2016. Dynamic mode decomposition with reproducing kernels for Koopman spectral analysis. *Advances in Neural Information Processing Systems*, **29**, 911–919.

Koopman, Bernard. 1931. Hamiltonian systems and transformation in Hilbert space. *Proceedings of the National Academy of Sciences of the United States of America*, **17**(5), 315–318.

Korda, Milan, and Mezić, Igor. 2018. Linear predictors for nonlinear dynamical systems: Koopman operator meets model predictive control. *Automatica*, **93**, 149–160.

Kou, Shauying, Elliott, David, and Tarn, Tzyh Jong. 1973. Observability of nonlinear systems. *Information and Control*, **22**(1), 89–99.

Kutz, J. Nathan, Brunton, Steven, Brunton, Bingni, and Proctor, Joshua. 2016a. *Dynamic Mode Decomposition: Data-Driven Modeling of Complex Systems*. SIAM.

Kutz, J. Nathan, Proctor, Joshua, and Brunton, Steven. 2018. Applied Koopman theory for partial differential equations and data-driven modeling of spatio-temporal systems. *Complexity*, **2018**, 6010634.

Kutz, J. Nathan, Proctor, Joshua, and Brunton, Steven. 2016b. Koopman theory for partial differential equations. *arXiv:1607.07076*.

Langley, Pat, Bradshaw, Gary, and Simon, Herbert. 1981. BACON. 5: The discovery of conservation laws. Pages 121–126 of *International Joint Conference on Artificial Intelligence*, vol. 1. Citeseer.

Li, Qianxiao, Dietrich, Felix, Bollt, Erik, and Kevrekidis, Ioannis. 2017. Extended dynamic mode decomposition with dictionary learning: A data-driven adaptive spectral decomposition of the Koopman operator. *Chaos: An Interdisciplinary Journal of Nonlinear Science*, **27**(10), 103111.

Lu, Hannah, and Tartakovsky, Daniel. 2020. Prediction accuracy of dynamic mode decomposition. *SIAM Journal on Scientific Computing*, **42**(3), A1639–A1662.

Mairal, Julien, Bach, Francis, Ponce, Jean et al. 2014a. Spams: A sparse modeling software, v2.6. http://spams-devel. gforge.inria. fr/downloads.html.

Mairal, Julien, Bach, Francis, Ponce, Jean, et al. 2014b. Sparse modeling for image and vision processing. *Foundations and Trends® in Computer Graphics and Vision*, **8**(2–3), 85–283.

Mauroy, Alexandre. 2021. Koopman operator theory for infinite-dimensional systems: Extended dynamic mode decomposition and identification of nonlinear PDEs. *Mathematics*, **9**(19), 2495. *arXiv:2103.12458*.

Mauroy, Alexandre, Mezić, Igor, and Moehlis, Jeff. 2013. Isostables, isochrons, and Koopman spectrum for the action–angle representation of stable fixed point dynamics. *Physica D: Nonlinear Phenomena*, **261**, 19–30.

Mauroy, Alexandre, Susuki, Y, and Mezić, I. 2020. *The Koopman Operator in Systems and Control*. Springer.

Mezić, Igor. 2005. Spectral properties of dynamical systems, model reduction and decompositions. *Nonlinear Dynamics*, **41**(1), 309–325. https://doi.org/10.1007/s11071-005-2824-x.

Nakao, Hiroya, and Mezić, Igor. 2020. Spectral analysis of the Koopman operator for partial differential equations. *Chaos: An Interdisciplinary Journal of Nonlinear Science*, **30**(11), 113131.

Otto, Samuel, and Rowley, Clarence. 2021. Koopman operators for estimation and control of dynamical systems. *Annual Review of Control, Robotics, and Autonomous Systems*, **4**, 59–87.

Pan, Shaowu, Arnold-Medabalimi, Nicholas, and Duraisamy, Karthik. 2021. Sparsity-promoting algorithms for the discovery of informative Koopman-invariant subspaces. *Journal of Fluid Mechanics*, **917**, A18. doi:https://doi.org/10.1017/jfm.2021.271.

Rudy, Samuel, Brunton, Steven, Proctor, Joshua, and Kutz, J. Nathan. 2017. Data-driven discovery of partial differential equations. *Science Advances*, **3**(4), e1602614.

Schmid, Peter. 2010. Dynamic mode decomposition of numerical and experimental data. *Journal of Fluid Mechanics*, **656**, 5–28.

Schmidt, Michael, and Lipson, Hod. 2009. Distilling free-form natural laws from experimental data. *Science*, **324**(5923), 81–85.

Tu, Jonathan, Rowley, Clarence, Luchtenburg, Dirk, Brunton, Steven, and Kutz, J. Nathan. 2013. On dynamic mode decomposition: Theory and applications. *Journal of Computational Dynamics*, **1**(2), 391–421. *arXiv:1312.0041*.

Valmorbida, Giorgio, and Anderson, James. 2017. Region of attraction estimation using invariant sets and rational Lyapunov functions. *Automatica*, **75**(January), 37–45.

Venturi, Daniele, and Dektor, Alec. 2021. Spectral methods for nonlinear functionals and functional differential equations. *Research in the Mathematical Sciences*, **8**(2), 1–39.

Williams, Matthew, Hemati, Maziar, Dawson, Scott, Kevrekidis, Ioannis, and Rowley, Clarence. 2016. Extending data-driven Koopman analysis to actuated systems. *IFAC-PapersOnLine*, **49**(18), 704–709.

Williams, Matthew, Kevrekidis, Ioannis, and Rowley, Clarence 2015a. A data-driven approximation of the Koopman operator: Extending dynamic mode decomposition. *Journal of Nonlinear Science*, **25**(6), 1307–1346.

Williams, Matthew, Rowley, Clarence, Mezić, Igor, and Kevrekidis, Ioannis. 2015b. Data fusion via intrinsic dynamic variables: An application of data-driven Koopman spectral analysis. *Europhysics Letters*, **109**(4), 40007.

Acknowledgments

This work was supported by the EU Horizon 2020 research and innovation program (grant NoMADS No. 777826), by the Israeli Science Foundation (grant ISF 534/19) and by the Ollendorff Minerva Center at the Technion – IIT. We would like to thank Prof. Gershon Wolansky from the Department of Mathematics, Technion and Dr. Eli Appelboim from the Electrical and Computer Engineering Department, and Dan Glaubach for stimulating discussions.

Cambridge Elements

Non-local Data Interactions: Foundations and Applications

About the Series

This series provides a mathematical description of the modelling, the analysis and the optimisation aspects of processing data that features complex and non-local relationships. It is intended for both students and researchers wishing to deepen their understanding of non-local analysis and explore applications to image and data processing.

Cambridge Elements

Non-local Data Interactions: Foundations and Applications

Elements in the Series

Generalized Normalizing Flows via Markov Chains
Gabriele Steidl, Paul Lyonel Hagemann and Johannes Hertrich

Nonlocal Continuum Limits of p*-Laplacian Problems on Graphs*
Imad El Bouchairi, Jalal M. Fadili, Yosra Hafiene and Abderrahim Elmoataz

Latent Modes of Nonlinear Flows: A Koopman Theory Analysis
Ido Cohen and Guy Gilboa

A full series listing is available at: www.cambridge.org/ENDI

Printed in the United States
by Baker & Taylor Publisher Services